"A timely corrective to the separatist, revisio en's movement that have been widely shai erful, moving revelation of courageous wo. ....o broke through the racial divide in an effort to forge a better world for all women. Bonnets and petticoats notwithstanding, these trailblazing visionaries were never the weaker sex!"

—KANYERE EATON, Senior Pastor, Fellowship Covenant Church

"An inspiring story of what activism and strategic grassroots philanthropy generated on behalf of freedom and justice 180 years ago, and against great odds. Great women forged the path before us, deploying their money to advance justice."

—JOSH MAILMAN and MONICA WINSOR,
activist philanthropists, Serious Change

"A galvanizing accounting of our collective history as Americans and a blueprint for where we must go next."

—DIANE WHITTY, Global Head of Philanthropy, JP Morgan

"Helen—a pioneer in the women's funding movement—is the perfect messenger to remind us on whose shoulders we stand as we work to create a world with equality and justice. Reading *And the Spirit Moved Them* is an opportunity to harness the strength, outrage, and protest from feminists in our past."

—ANA L. OLIVEIRA, President and CEO,
The New York Women's Foundation

"Helen LaKelly Hunt's compelling historical narrative on the rise of feminism in America reveals that faith, women and men working in partnership, and healthy relationships were the foundation of the female abolitionist's organizing. Their relational style of movement building is a blueprint for healing culture today."

—ELIZABETH and KEVIN PHILLIPS, Phillips Foundation,
Cocreators, Healthy Relationship Initiative, Greensboro, NC

"I care a great deal about and work to help propagate global feminism and environmentalism. The abolitionist feminists broke free of their cultural confinement to the domestic sphere, finding a public voice with which to help others. Hunt's book reveals the diversity beating at the heart of our abolitionist and feminist histories, giving these women the audience they so richly deserve. *And the Spirit Moved Them* is a model for working in partnership—with passion, power, and protest—to unleash a vision for a healthy and sustainable future."

—TREA C. YIP, TY Commercial Group, Inc.

"Helen LaKelly Hunt brings us a little-known but profoundly moving story from the annals of American history. It is a story that needs to be told, now more than ever before; a story of sisterhood that is as deeply spiritual as it is political, that defied the racial barriers of its day to create a movement with lasting impact. More than a century later, let their brave and fierce voices no longer be lost to history."

—SERENE JONES, President, Union Theological Seminary

"Fine historical research pushes us to probe even more deeply into the past and surprises us with its contemporary relevance. This absorbing book reminds us that women of resonant religious faith then and now fulfill their faith commitments by propelling our basic human freedoms."

—BONNIE WHEELER, historian,
Southern Methodist University

"Raised in Honduras, I came to the US to get a college education and worked to achieve my professional goals, eventually becoming a VP at Goldman Sachs. I benefitted greatly from the faith-fueled efforts of these early abolitionist women. This is an important piece of history urgently needed. I have great admiration and gratitude for Helen LaKelly Hunt for this book."

—MARIA CHRIN, Cofounder, Circle Financial

"Faith, feminism, voice, movement building, money, power. These are words that are not often connected—but they should be. Used together they will take us further, faster, in the struggle for gender equality. Helen's book bridges the past with the present. By sharing the stories of the earliest feminist leaders, Hunt invites us to own our own power in the quest for true equality."

—JACKI ZEHNER, Founding Chair and CEO,
Women Moving Millions

"Relationships anchored by an interwoven vision are the catalytic currency to sustainable change. Too many world changers stay in the shadows of history, making this spotlight on the visionary abolitionist women deeply significant. They collaborated cross-race, cross-class, in solidarity, using relational organizing so desperately needed in today's polarized society. These women travailed until they birthed a movement. We applaud the vision and the passion of *And the Spirit Moved Them!*"

—OLANIKKI and TORREY CARROLL, Ambassadors,
Safe Conversations, Relationships First

"Helen LaKelly Hunt is both a scholar and a practitioner of feminism. As she recreates the determination of the early feminists in this book, and models this energy in her own life, she brings many of us along with her."

— CECILIA GUTHRIE BOONE and CYNTHIA YUNG,
The Boone Family Foundation

"These stories can't be hidden any longer, just as we can no longer deny the bias and prejudice that resides so deeply in our systems, culture, and ourselves. Thank you, Helen LaKelly Hunt, for discovering and bringing forth the contribution of these women, willing to risk all to stand for justice and human dignity."

—LAUREN EMBREY, President,
Embrey Family Foundation: Dallas Faces Race Initiative

"As women continue to break through social barriers today, these nineteenth-century abolitionist women offer insights that can help guide our global society into the future."

—VINCE POSCENTE, *The Age of Speed*

"Helen LaKelly Hunt combines new historical scholarship on feminism with key insights from Imago Theory, a relational therapy co-created with her husband. The result is a spellbinding work that retells the history of American feminism in ways that have implications for equality movements everywhere."

—KIERSTEN MAREK, Past Senior Editor,
Inside Philanthropy; Founder, *Philanthropy Women*

"In her wonderful new book, Helen LaKelly Hunt brings to life a lost chapter in American history of great historical importance—and of direct relevance to our turbulent times. It shows how, working together across race and class, women can challenge entrenched beliefs justifying domination and injustice. I highly recommend this beautifully written book for everyone, young and old."

—RIANE EISLER, *The Chalice and the Blade*

"Helen LaKelly Hunt has a rare talent for illuminating lost chapters of history. In *And the Spirit Moved Them*, she sheds light on the little-known intersectional beginnings of American feminism, reminding us that human relationships lie at the heart of every lasting social movement. This is a story to be shared with all the women in your life."

—SHEILA C. JOHNSON, CEO, Salamander Hotels
and Resorts; Cofounder, BET

"We may never know why Elizabeth Cady Stanton and Susan B. Anthony chose to start their history of women's suffrage with Seneca Falls, not the earlier convention of abolitionist suffragists who fought against cruelties imposed by race and sex, but thanks to the revelations in *And the Spirit Moved Them,* this crucial and inspiring history is no longer lost to us. A must read for all who care about the past and present intertwining of sex and race—in other words, who care about human rights."　　　　　—GLORIA STEINEM, activist and author

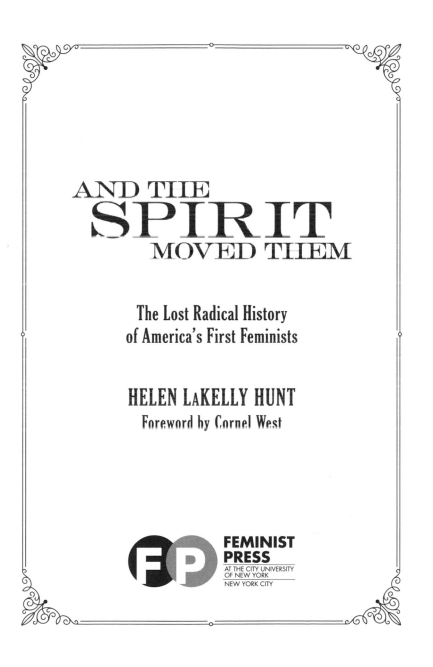

AND THE
SPIRIT
MOVED THEM

The Lost Radical History
of America's First Feminists

HELEN LaKELLY HUNT
Foreword by Cornel West

FEMINIST PRESS
AT THE CITY UNIVERSITY
OF NEW YORK
NEW YORK CITY

Published in 2017 by the Feminist Press
at the City University of New York
The Graduate Center
365 Fifth Avenue, Suite 5406
New York, NY 10016

feministpress.org

First Feminist Press edition 2017

NEW YORK | Council on
STATE OF
OPPORTUNITY. | the Arts

This book was made possible thanks to a grant from New York State Council
on the Arts with the support of Governor Andrew Cuomo and the New York
State Legislature.

Third printing February 2018

Cover design by Drew Stevens
Text design by Suki Boynton

Library of Congress Cataloging-in-Publication Data is available for this title.

This book is dedicated to:

*Kathryn Ruth, Kimberly June, and Leah Grace,
our daughters who live out daily, with an adamant
passion similar to the abolitionist feminists, the
faith, relationality, and commitment to the least
of these, hoping to heal our broken culture.*

o o o

*Our son Hunter, gifted in both music
and philosophy, who contributes artfully
toward cultural transformation.*

o o o

*And, of course, Harville, whose powerful theories
for couples are also furthering the global feminist
vision of a more relational world.*

CONTENTS

ACKNOWLEDGMENTS

A special group of women around me grew to love the women of this book and helped me hold on to their stories. Sally K. Lindsey assisted me with research and graphics. Joan Denniston, Bernadette Gallegos, Elizabeth Perrachione, and Rachel Meltzer each helped in special ways to bring these stories into the light.

Special thanks to Catherine Whitney for helping so much in the final stages. I am grateful to Cornel West for reading this manuscript and then responding with his beautiful foreword.

Four women have been spiritual mentors. Gloria Steinem, who will hate me for writing this, but in addition to her visionary brilliance, is an absolute saint. Gloria has always been my North Star. Second, Betty Friedan, who very early on, when feminism was so secular, encouraged me in my vision of faith and feminism. Third, the Reverend Kanyere Eaton, the strategic, passionate director of the Sister Fund, who took my interest in faith-based feminism and helped it spread in countries throughout the globe. And fourth, Annie Sales, a nanny in our family, whose heart of strength and love has been an inspiration.

And then, a list of my sister activists: the dynamic Jacki Zehner of Women Moving Millions, the wondrous Ana Oliveira at the New York Women's Foundation, and Maria Chrin, who works to empower women around money; as well as Tracy Gary, Chris Grumm, Jess Houssian, and new leaders such as Courtney Harvey. Each has helped strengthen a faith-based and relational feminism in the service of greater justice, taking up the banner from our early foremothers.

Above all, it is an honor to acknowledge Jennifer Baumgardner, the executive director of the Feminist Press. She took in this manuscript when it was an orphaned newborn. She knew how to cradle it, nurture it, and grow it into the book you have in your hands. Her passion and vision has moved the brave, world-changing abolitionist feminists out of the darkness of a lost history and into the light, where their genius and vision can now shine. May we celebrate the unveiling of these abolitionist feminists together.

Thanks as well to the Feminist Press team, Alyea Canada, Drew Stevens, Suki Boynton, Jisu Kim, Wren Hanks, Lauren Hook, Hannah Goodwin, and Lucia Brown.

FOREWORD

HOLY INDIGNATION

This powerful and poignant book narrates the unique intersection of the two greatest social movements in nineteenth-century America: abolitionism and feminism. Author Helen LaKelly Hunt is uniquely attuned to these women—many lost to history—whose courage provided a "sacred blueprint" for the intersectional feminism advocated today, nearly two centuries later.

Hunt gets inside the hearts, minds, and souls of the major black and white leaders and activists through detailed and meticulous engagement with their letters, journals, and other writings. Her research reveals three surprises: first, the profoundly religious roots of the early abolitionists and feminists; second, the interracial character of this early feminism; and third, the relational content of their revolutionary activism. The "holy duty" and the "holy indignation" of these female activists focused dually on slavery and patriarchy. Their bold organizing created loyalty to each other, which sustained them in the face of death threats and character assassination. Their faith and relationships led them to exemplify some of the highest profiles in courage ever in American history. And yet, most Americans know almost nothing of these women. Tragically they were written out of history, and without their example we might believe the women's movement began at Seneca Falls in 1838 and without black women.

I'm grateful that this book can begin to correct the record. Still, it is Hunt's pioneering historical synthesis of race and gender, faith and feminism, justice and spirituality for which I'm most grateful. She never loses sight of the profoundly human relationships and personal bonds that constitute social movements. She skillfully weaves together the complex connections between structures and agency, institutions and action, against the backdrop of "empathetic attunement"—the love and sisterhood— of her "holy warriors."

You'll soon be meeting these grand examples of meaningful activism, and I hope learning of them stays with you as much as it has me. Among them, such giants as Sarah and Angelina Grimké (of white aristocratic origins), Grace and Sarah Douglass (of free black beginnings), Lydia Maria Child and Abby Kelley Foster (writers of white middle-class status), and Lucretia Mott and Mary Grew (of white Quaker and Baptist backgrounds) take us to the moral core and spiritual essence—that is, to the raw stuff—that kept the abolitionist and feminist movements going in the face of hatred and hostility.

The messages contained herein are timeless—but they couldn't be more timely. The global movements for truth, justice, freedom, and equality today so badly need the kind of courage, empathy, bonds, humility, and spiritual fortitude of these "holy warriors." We all can be grateful that the spirit moved Helen LaKelly Hunt to write this wise book about our American foremothers.

—CORNEL WEST, 2017

INTRODUCTION
HER VOICE, HER PEN, HER PURSE

*We abolition women are turning the world
upside down.*

ANGELINA GRIMKÉ

Some years ago, as I was doing research for my
PhD, I found myself crouched on the basement
floor of the Barnard Library in New York City. And as I was
crawling along the lowest shelves of old history books,
my hand found a small booklet. Pages that had once
been white were now yellowed with age. Carefully pick-
ing it up, I saw that it was a set of minutes detailing the
proceedings of a women's convention in the early 1800s.
"Ah, Seneca Falls," I nodded to myself. As a longtime feminist and activist, I knew the Seneca Falls Convention in

1848 was considered to be the birthplace of the American women's rights movement.

I looked more carefully at the cover. The title read, *Turning the World Upside Down: The Anti-Slavery Convention of American Women Held in New York City, May 9–12, 1837*. I felt confused. Was there another national women's convention during this era that I'd never heard of? As I scanned the slim volume that next hour, I came to realize that I'd stumbled upon evidence, the first I'd seen, that abolitionist women—black and white together—helped catalyze a social revolution eleven years before the "official" beginning of the American women's rights movement. Odd, I thought.

Digging deeper over the next few months, I learned that when Elizabeth Cady Stanton was writing the first history of the American women's rights movement, abolitionist feminist Lucretia Mott wrote to her in 1855, saying, "Let me suggest then, that the opening Chapter go farther back than [1848]. . . . From the time of the 1st. Convention of Women—in New Y[ork] 1837—the battle began." Stanton chose not to act on Lucretia's suggestion, opting to christen the Seneca Falls Convention as the beginning of the women's rights movement in the United States. And that's the way the story has been told for over one hundred years. The 1837 Anti-Slavery Convention organized by women and for women was all but forgotten, a mere footnote in history. As I read on, I began to wonder if Lucretia Mott had it right. I had to know more. But little did I imagine that my discovery would yield such rich rewards.

IN 1837 ALL things seemed possible for the collective of women who gathered together in New York City with a stated aspiration to change the world. They were determined that their cause, the abolition of slavery, must become the law. Angelina Grimké wrote at the time, "It is my deep, solemn, deliberate conviction, that *this is a cause worth dying for.*" Even she was not conscious of how this women's revolt against the moral crime of slavery would eventually seed the movement for women's own emancipation.

The women who attended the first Anti-Slavery Convention of American Women were determined to right the sin of slavery perpetuated by their country. They sought to reconcile the profound idealism of American rhetoric with the cruel values expressed in its reality. After all, nine of the first twelve presidents owned slaves, despite speaking eloquently about the rights of all to life, liberty, and the pursuit of happiness. To the women in this book, slavery was an abomination of God's law. Having no political voice, however, and being relegated to the private realm of their homes, these women raised a cry that shook the foundations of the old order. "I know you do not make the laws," Angelina Grimké wrote to women across the country, "but I also know that you are the wives and mothers, the sisters and daughters of those who do; and if you really suppose you can do nothing to overthrow slavery, you are greatly mistaken." One at a time, women courageously stepped up to join Angelina—forming what became a small, impassioned army of activists. And they stormed the public stage to speak out against the atrocities of slavery. The Anti-Slavery Convention catapulted these women into the public sphere and, for a while, captured the attention of the nation.

But equally remarkable as their determination to act so boldly together was their ability to organize their vision into a practical blueprint for change. Their convention bound together and reconceived the social, racial, and gender issues of the day, becoming the foundation of a new social order—one that exemplified the values of equality and justice. Without knowing it, the women also designed a dynamic model for movement building that could be relevant for our global women's movement today.

This blueprint, for which they've never been credited, was defined by three factors:

1. The abolitionist feminist movement building in the 1830s was inclusive—across race, class, and socioeconomic status. Most striking was the interracial character of their meetings, especially considering that the male abolitionist societies of the time were all white. Yet, the abolitionist feminists knew their movement needed to be *with* not *for*—and thus inclusive of— African American women. As the poet Sarah Forten wrote on the cover of the convention materials, "Our 'skins may differ,' but from thee we claim / a sister's privilege, in a sister's name."[1] Rather than white women seeking to work "on behalf of" black women, white women worked

alongside black women, arm in arm, as human beings, in an egalitarianism that was nonexistent elsewhere at the time. Black women initiated this movement and helped preside over the 1837 convention. Black and white women together drafted, debated, and adopted their resolutions. Thus, while the Seneca Falls Convention of 1848 had only white women present, it was a deeply committed interracial group of women that first catalyzed American women's revolutionary spirit.

2. The movement was "relational," knit together and informed by the strong personal bonds they formed. As a sisterhood, they broke through the silence of social conventions by emphasizing the importance of solidarity. They thought of themselves not as individuals but as "selves-in-relation." Theirs was social reform that did not rely on an "us vs. them" mentality. I think of this today, when there are several powerful movements at play speaking to the lives of black men and women, including Black Lives Matter and sacred efforts to abolish the prison industrial system. Because of my knowledge of these early feminists, I understand what the call "black lives matter" means: that no lives matter unless black lives matter. When society would separate the abolitionist women, or when they themselves were in disagreement, they looked for ways to have "both/and" and unite with in-

clusion. They strove for all to be at the table arm in arm, in relationship.

Focusing on the issue of slavery, the abolitionist feminists practiced empathy at their weekly sewing circles, learning "sympathy for the slave," which became a key tenet of their movement. While the women were sewing, each took a turn standing up to read a passage from a slave narrative. They struggled to put themselves in a position to feel what it was like to be auctioned off and owned, to be separated from one's children or parents or spouse. "Let every slaveholder apply these queries to his own heart," Angelina Grimké challenged them. "Am *I* willing to be a slave? Am *I* willing to see my mother a slave, or my father, my sister, or my brother?" This is one of the many ways the women strove to make their organizing personal, relational, and informed by empathy.

3. Their movement building was in large part a faith-fueled activism. The abolitionist women were able to separate God's overarching message of love from the institutionalized practices of churches that condoned slavery. The tenets of the Christian faith—mercy, love, and the power of the Resurrection—catalyzed them into action toward universal justice and peace. At the time, the common belief was that women were the keepers of the moral flame. They were charged with instilling morality inside the home, and for the most part they accepted this identity, even

as it kept them subjugated. But the abolitionist women took that sense of moral authority
out into the world, calling their work a "holy
duty." At their convention, the women declared,
"We wield no other sword than the sword of
the Spirit; we encounter the foes of freedom
with the word of God, whilst our feet are shod
with the preparation of the Gospel of peace. . . .
[W]e know that truth is might and will prevail."
They claimed equality for themselves, using the
same theological assumptions to claim equality
for their sisters and brothers in the slave states.
While this put them in direct opposition to the
prevailing religious dogmas of the day, they believed they were on "a sacred mission." For many
women, black and white, it was their passionate
faith in God that unleashed their revolutionary
social activism.

Equality, relatedness, and a faith-inspired vision were
the bonding material of the abolitionist women's movement. With these powerful tenets, they boldly challenged
the hypocrisy in their culture. They sought to heal the
ethical dissonance that was tearing apart their country.
They saw that this split consciousness was causing otherwise well-intended citizens, people who desired to be
good, to behave inhumanely. They drew on everything
they had to combat hypocrisy's greatest manifestation—
slavery. In challenging slavery, finding their voice, and
establishing ways to organize and fund their movement,
the women created a rubric that began to change their

world. And this organizing methodology seemed so visionary and transformational, I realized it was one that could help contribute to ours today.

Discovering this glorious sisterhood, long lost in that dark and dusty archive of a library, my heart soared. It felt very personal to me. The window on history that I opened in the Barnard Library unsealed a parallel window into my past. I was struck by how these women spoke to my journey—how I'd learned, just as they had, that power was not given but stepped into, and that its full expression occurred in the arenas of voice, money, empowerment, solidarity, and faith. They were, in effect, telling me *my* story. And I longed to tell theirs.

I GREW UP in a prominent Texas oil family. My childhood, while abundant in material resources, was emotionally unsafe and confusing. As was true of many families in the fifties, my father was the dictator of the house. Mom always called Dad "Popsie," and she took on the duties of doting wife and devoted mother. Dad made the house rules. The only television show we were allowed to watch was *Father Knows Best*. True story.

Years later, I was reading nursery rhymes to my children and found myself saying from "Sing a Song of Sixpence":

> The King is in his counting house
> counting out his money.
> The Queen is in the parlor
> eating bread and honey.

What an epiphany! That is exactly how I was taught to handle money; specifically, I wasn't taught to handle it at all and was kept out of the action. In my patriarchal family, my father knew what assets we had, how to access them, and where we'd deploy that money. My mother, sisters, and I were left in the parlor with our good manners and allowances. Echoing the defined gender roles of the early abolitionists, my brother was groomed to take over the family oil business. My sisters and I were taught to be precious Southern belles and marry men who would act as our proxies in building the family fortune.

An obedient product of my upbringing, I was fine with this role differentiation. So when my father invited my fiancé, Randy, into the wood-paneled domain of his office to discuss the family business and my resources, I felt only the smallest ripple of unease. He had never told *me* about them. Neither of my parents had ever talked to me about the family business or money, and presumably my mother knew very little herself. In Texas, in the 1970s, one did not use the words "women" and "money" in the same sentence. Although the women of my era had gained the right to vote long ago, the overall ecosystem I lived in had many similarities to the one feminist abolitionists inhabited—a realm where women of all races and classes experienced having no power or voice. No wonder I was so captivated by these women who had declared their right to shout out against slavery and claim their own authority. I lived a modern-day version of their lives. It would take me many years to find my own voice and awaken to my own power.

Back then, I dutifully followed my mother's lead. I even learned how to curtsy. Inside, however, seeds of revolt were being planted and taking root in the depths of my heart. An early epiphany occurred when I served as a camp counselor through our church, First Baptist. Until then, I had only experienced the church as homogenous, with all faces during worship looking like mine. First Baptist had two separate services—one for white people and one for people of color. The church camp, in contrast, was integrated and richly diverse. Like the early abolitionists, I was deeply uncomfortable living in segregation, but I didn't have the language or experience to give expression to my unease. Working as a counselor, I realized that it wasn't my elegant white-only girls' school, the mansion I lived in, or the possessions I owned that mattered. Rather, it was being part of the diverse youth of this camp that was the most joyful, worthwhile aspect of my childhood. It had never occurred to me before that there were many ways of being fulfilled—or that I could find such value in the lives of people who were not like me. In the disenfranchised parts of society were places where mutual respect, interconnectivity, and love could flourish. I blossomed in that environment, and I felt my destiny unfolding—a very different destiny than my family had in mind for me.

Another spark of rebellion came after I was married. I took a job as a teacher in an inner-city high school in Dallas, although my husband said this was "crazy." I felt so at home being able to interact with these students, but the reality was that they lacked most of the basic books and supplies available in the all-white public school where I'd done my student teaching. In their midst I felt a new impulse born within me—a yearning toward justice. I saw that the students of color needed access to resources that the white students had in order for us to do our job, as teachers and as members of this country. As clear as the abolitionist feminists felt called to their work by God, I heard His announcement of my calling and mission. I felt I had to do something about the inequality I was witnessing, but I wasn't sure what or how. I stopped teaching when I became pregnant, and our daughters, Kathryn and Kim, were born over the next two years. I was a stay-at-home mom, living in a lovely, safe neighborhood, but I kept inside me a deep anxiety about the terrible dichotomy inherent in my life. The mothers living in poverty in other parts of Dallas loved their children as much as I loved our daughters, but they did not have the resources to help them receive even a basic education. I thought of how I might be able to help them.

My burgeoning intentions did not square with the other side of my life—the one where my husband worked among the riches of my family fortune. The husband who was "representing" me at the company fell in with my half brothers, and together they decided to corner the silver market—a goal I never would have had for our family money. It was heartbreaking to realize the man I'd married was working in such opposition to who I was in my soul. While I was imagining the good we could do with our resources, my husband and half brothers were concerned mainly with amassing a greater fortune.

It was a wake-up call for me. I saw clearly that *I* had not sent Randy to the company to be my proxy—but society had. Randy's work had become 24/7, and his trading screen was in his home office. I was beginning to feel extinguished in our marriage; my values weren't represented anywhere in it. I had to find my voice. I went to therapy, trying to find a way I could be strong in my marriage. Randy's work fell apart; I began pursuing independent interests, including studying psychology. Eventually we both agreed divorce was best. What made me confident about the repercussions for the children was that I knew in my heart my daughters would never respect me if I were only an appendage of my husband.

In 1979 I moved to New York City and set out to find a personal financial mentor. I needed to learn about money. I was longing to find the knowledge of my identity that had been denied me my whole life. Recalling it, I am reminded of Angelina Grimké's poignant question: "Can you not see that women could do and would do a hundred times more for the slave, if she were not fettered?" I, too, had to break free of the shackles of obedience and propriety that hobbled me. And like the abolitionist feminists, my longing for these things was sparked by a need to honor the self God created me to be, a woman in a high-net-worth family, and to take control of that power, rather than deny it. So my life became structured. Monday through Friday mornings, I dropped my daughters off at the Catholic school I had chosen to instill values in them. I was heartened that the Catholic Church honored the Mother of God, thereby honoring all women and the vocation of motherhood in critically important ways, which for a Baptist was a radical thing to do. I then took a taxi to the Morgan Stanley offices and watched my mentor trade until it was time to pick the girls up. I learned option trading like Randy. To learn more about the family company I read annual reports of other oil companies and spoke to others in the industry. I began option trading on my own. At that time there was a bubble, and my trading did very well! Suddenly I had money that I'd made on my own, money that I felt was truly *mine,* and that I felt I could give away. My life as a donor began.

ONE DAY I got a call from my sister, Swance. "Helen, do you have a current copy of *Forbes* handy?" she asked. "*We're rich!*" Sure enough, as I opened to the page Swance indicated, I saw my name with a notation about how much I was worth. I was stunned. No one had ever discussed our financial status with my sisters or me, and here I was listed as one of the wealthiest individuals in the world. I'm aware that it might seem ludicrous that we could have been so dissociated from this massive fortune, but all of the women in the family were. After all, money isn't polite to talk about. I felt foolish and even disoriented at the time, but I've since learned that my experience is a common one for females in high-net-worth families. Nancy Drew had been my favorite fictional character as a teen, and at that moment, I vowed to adopt her sleuthing powers. My sisters and I began asking questions, learning about the trust configuration. Over the years, those at the company had asked each of us separately what would be a comfortable amount for us to live on each month, and we received that as an allowance. Finding out the extent of the wealth woke us from our deeply socialized behavior. My sisters and I had begun to reflect on the bread and honey we'd been fed, and decided it was time to enter the counting house.

My voice, I realized, was linked with my mission and a deep abiding sense of personal responsibility. I held the message of the Gospel of Luke within my heart: "To whom much is given, much is expected." Ultimately, my sisters and I gained the ability to participate in company profits. And with this, we could begin to invest in society and contribute to the Hunt legacy in a meaningful way that reflected *our* values, too. I took one step at a time down my path into an unknown future.

WITH OUR NEWFOUND access to money, Swanee and I attended a Council on Foundations meeting in 1983. Swanee, the extrovert, attended as many sessions and events as she could, and I, the introvert, went to an area designated for all the foundations to display copies of their annual reports. I knew little about philanthropy at the time (not even that it translates from the Latin as "love for humanity"), so I gathered up about sixty reports and went back to my room to read them. I noted that all the boards of directors were composed of white men with distinguished titles and bios.

Near the end of the second day, one document arrested my attention. It was the first annual report from the San Francisco Women's Fund, and I was shocked as I read every word and absorbed each photo. Women from all racial and socioeconomic backgrounds were represented on the board, their voices unleashed. Grants were awarded to frontline organizations deeply grounded in their communities, focusing on the empowerment of women

and girls. Imagine women not just being pretty append-
ages to the males in their lives! Tears started streaming
down my cheeks. Reminded of my formative experience
at the First Baptist camp, I thought, "Oh, isn't this amazing? A foundation whose governing structure matches
the ideals it espouses. What a brilliant concept. This feels
like what I was meant to do!"

The timing of my revelation was significant. In the
1970s, a shockwave was coursing through women's activist circles. Newly released statistics showed that women
shouldered a vastly disproportionate burden of poverty,
yet a mere 2 *percent* of our nation's foundation dollars
was directed to programs for women and girls. In fact,
philanthropic organizations in the United States had
no designation for women's causes. The closest a donor
could come to funding women's advancement was "girls'"
education. Gloria Steinem, Shirley Chisholm, Betty
Friedan, and so many others were publicly inciting the
second wave of feminism at the same time that women
across the nation were building the political and emotional resources needed to support their movement. A
small band of women had the vision to prioritize funding
feminism. They wanted a philanthropy that grew side by
side with their activism. And thus women's funds—and,
in time, a whole new field of philanthropy—was born.
These funds would come to have great meaning for me.
I was overcome by the vision of an organizing principle
that put "women" and "money" in the same sentence to
further the love of humanity. Imagine, I thought, chan-
neling money to lift up the mothers I met in the poorer
parts of Dallas—and mothers like them everywhere.

Three organizations helped usher in a new model of philanthropy: the Ms. Foundation; Mama Cash, a fund in Amsterdam; and the Astraea Lesbian Foundation for Justice. Women's funds sounded a wake-up call in the early 1980s, explicitly inviting privileged women to step up, *own* their power, and write (bigger and bigger) checks for the advancement of women everywhere. In contrast to philanthropy run by men, the boards of women's funds had cross-race, cross-class, and cross-socioeconomic representation. Frontline activists and donors sat side by side. What the women's funds were doing was revolutionary. Though it was a radical departure, the pairing of donors and activists proved exceedingly effective in tackling many of the issues these funds sought to address. The feminist mantra that women are the experts of their own lives was applied to the allocation of money.

It was nothing less than a democratization of philanthropy, and these women's funds began to multiply into a global network. In 1980 there were seven women's funds. Five years later this number had grown to thirty-two. The Women's Funding Network (WFN) emerged in 1985 to shepherd these fledgling foundations. By 1990 a total of fifty-seven women's funds dotted the landscape, and in 1997 there were close to one hundred. In 2014 more than one hundred and sixty women's funds had spread into thirty countries, spanning six continents. In the early eighties, I met Tracy Gary, the author of *Inspired Philanthropy* and a key mother of the women's funding movement, and brought her to Texas to help birth the Dallas Women's Foundation. Soon after, I was asked to join the board of the Ms. Foundation while also helping to found the New York Women's Foundation and Women's Funding Network, among others. I was part of a small army, traveling the country to encourage those who wanted to start women's funds in their own communities. This spontaneous expansion clearly indicated a zeitgeist, and yet, even with this growing global presence, women's funds remained largely undercapitalized. It nagged at me.

The more I networked, the more something dawned on me—the disconnect between money and women. One might assume that all women of wealth have access to power. Sadly, this is untrue. As Gloria Steinem wrote in the *Trailblazers* booklet, "Wives and mothers within wealthy families are often expected, or even legally required, to cede power to family advisors and trusts. . . . It is so taken for granted that it's rarely even named as a major cause of the feminization of poverty."

More recently, the anthropologist Wednesday Martin, author of *Primates of Park Avenue*, chronicled wealthy women in New York who felt that they were only "allowed" to spend "their husband's money" on expensive clothing and services, rather than direct it to any cause they believed might make meaningful change in their lives and the lives of others.[2] I had heard the term "golden handcuffs" used to describe a form of bondage wealthy women were subjected to regarding their family's, and even their own, money—the very ceding of power I experienced. It might be hard to imagine if you haven't experienced this sense of impotence amid power, but it felt like a miracle that I'd broken away from the pattern and was slowly finding my voice. The more involved I became in the women's funding movement, the more I felt a responsibility to take full advantage of the position I was born into. Yes, I needed to take ownership of the resources I had available to me. And then, the most strategic thing I could do for others was to help other high-net-worth women wake up and step into their power by taking ownership of *their* family money. We were women close to power; we could shape that power.

Working collectively, each of us amplifying one another's voices and resources, meant this work could be as empowering and transformational for me and other women of wealth as it was for the frontline activists we were supporting. It meant that we could dream as big as Andrew Carnegie did when he funded the creation of nearly two thousand public libraries.

By the 1990s, much had changed regarding the status of women in society and the presence of women in philanthropy. Yet, one unfortunate statistic remained: for the most part, wealthy women failed to write big, bold checks for women's philanthropy. They might fund the symphony or their husband's alma mater at the million-dollar level, but a women's fund rarely received more than $30,000 to $50,000. This misguided generosity had a long history. In 1857 suffragist Matilda Joslyn Gage had lamented the failure of wealthy women to fund their own emancipation: "Why is it every day I read in the newspaper of another woman making bequests to yet another museum," she wrote, "but women fail to understand the cause that underlies all others in importance, *women's rights*?" At the time, the suffrage movement was in dire financial straits. "In this bleak moment," wrote Gage, "not a single woman of wealth stepped forward, pocketbook in hand.

. . . Is it not strange that women of wealth are constantly giving large sums of money to endow professorships and colleges for boys exclusively . . . and yet give no thought to their own sex—crushed in ignorance, poverty, and prostitution?"[3] Quietly, though, a few trailblazing women in my era had begun breaking with tradition and writing those million-dollar checks. I began collecting their stories for a history book I felt must be written about women funding their own futures. These women were making feminist history. I needed it to be preserved and understood, not lost.

One day Swanee called me. "Helen," she said, "I was revising my will and I don't want to wait until I am dead to give you money. If I assign this funding to you now, do you think you can help raise the bar on women's giving?" Now, with Swanee inspiring me with her money, I added a contribution of my own. I called Chris Grumm at the Women's Funding Network and we began to strategize a visionary philanthropic effort. Our goal was to raise $150 million from women for women over a two-year period— from April 2007 to May 2009. Donors were invited to pledge a million dollars or more within any of the global network of women's funds. And so, Women Moving Millions (WMM) was born.

"NEVER BEFORE IN the history of the world have women funded their own advancement, their own voice in society," wrote Kathleen McCarthy, from the Center for the Study of Philanthropy at the City University of New York, describing this work as "a new culture of giving." We titled the history I was writing *The Trailblazer Book*, and we continued to fill the pages with the passionate, but always (surprisingly) vulnerable, stories of each WMM donor. The book set the tone for the relational movement building I've since fully embraced and advocated. Stories are important; they unlock the heart and invite empathy and connection. "At last, I have found my tribe," more than one woman wrote as she sent in her check. "When can we meet each other in person?" Halfway to the goal, the country began to sink into what became a global financial crisis. Much to our surprise, this did not slow WMM down. Instead, over $182 million dollars was raised, with donors representing eight countries. Never before had women risen up to fund women at these unprecedented levels. The women kept sending their stories for *The Trailblazer Book*, and the checks continued to pour in.

Something new was happening. In the past, as I'd helped to found women's funds, it was always an uphill climb. I remembered how people laughed when we spoke about establishing the Dallas Women's Foundation. They said it would never happen. We received the same response when we worked diligently to start the New York Women's Foundation. We felt like we had to beg for each $10,000 or $50,000 check we received. I would say, "Thank you, thank you!" Yet with WMM, all we had to do was show them the book and make a request: "Would you like to make a pledge of a million or more?" More often than not, the donors would embrace me and say, with tears in their eyes, "Yes! Thank you, thank you so much!" I couldn't explain the shift of energy around giving. It was confusing and counterintuitive. I called Carol Gilligan, the noted women's psychologist, and said, "Carol, I don't understand. Why are the women thanking *me*?"

Carol's reply cut to the heart of it. She said, "You're helping to heal their dissociation. By writing those bold checks, they became associated to their own power." So many of the women claimed it was the *Trailblazer* history that spoke to them. "You can't be what you can't see" became a motto in our work. The women reading the stories of the other million-dollar donors saw their potential illuminated. My intuitive sense of the mutuality of empowerment was confirmed. As women of means were now capitalizing the funds within the women's funding movement, they were breaking free of their own golden handcuffs. My calling for justice had taken the form of liberating high-net-worth women to organize in wielding the kind of financial clout that builds, not just empires, but movements. The early abolitionist women would have been proud to see all this. They were the first feminists to appreciate the power of the purse, but their efforts were relegated to "womanly" endeavors—making quilts and baking pies to sell at market. We feminists were finally taking hold of the "purse"—the bank accounts and the funding within our trusts—and mobilizing our financial power.

Finding my voice around money and working with other women to find theirs gave me a platform that harkened back to the abolitionist women more than a century ago. Even before I found that pamphlet detailing their organizing, I had been heeding their call. Still, there remained one missing element before I could fully embrace my feminist calling.

AS AN ADULT, my entry into feminism returned to me parts of myself I had buried as a teenager. I grew more confident and creative: more able to say no, set boundaries, follow my inner compass, and stand up for myself. But there was one problem. There was a part of me I kept hidden from my activist sisters—the part that was Christian.

What began as a private sense that I should keep quiet about my faith was painfully affirmed at a Ms. Foundation board meeting in 1986. Each meeting began with a personal check-in. Without self-consciousness, women talked about debt, sex, and addiction, and others around the table listened graciously. At one meeting, lulled into the camaraderie, I told a brief story about a painful experience I was having. My sister board members were with me until I shared a Bible verse that transformed my view of my struggle:

> Therefore we do not lose heart. Though outwardly we are wasting away, yet inwardly we are being renewed day by day. For our momentary troubles are achieving for us an eternal glory that far outweighs them all. So we fix our eyes not on what is seen, but on what is unseen, since what is seen is temporary, but what is unseen is eternal.
> —2 Corinthians 4:16–18.

Suddenly, there was utter silence. A few cleared their throats. The message felt clear. There was no place for Jesus on the cross in modern feminism.

Part of me was humiliated. But I could also understand why some secular feminists were so suspicious of religion. With the dogma of many churches containing patriarchal values, organized religion has been no friend to women. Men hold the power in most churches throughout the world, and they've been slow to share it with women. Institutionalized religion can decimate the spirit.

At its essence, however, the Christian faith—like other faith traditions—can unleash a spirit of universal harmony, of self in community, and of connection, empathy, and radical love. The biblical charge to "love one another, contribute to the needs of others, live peaceably with all" is a sentiment embraced by every women's organization I've worked with, even if it isn't explicitly recognized as biblical. The mission of the women's movement, "peace on earth, good will to all women and men," shares the mission of Christianity. Jesus was a feminist. A feminist agape would be a powerful thing indeed.

I knew, too, that there were religious roots of American feminism that had been forgotten—or maybe never even fully articulated. For example, Elizabeth Cady Stanton toured Western Europe and visited monasteries. She was inspired by the way women ran these large institutions. The abbesses managed complex finances, officiated at meetings, and controlled the order of hundreds of people. Stanton had never seen a woman wield such power in the United States, and seeing the nuns emboldened her imagination about what women could do and be. Angelina Grimké had been inspired by the story of Joan of Arc. (Now *she* was a feminist!) For me, the wake-up call came in reading *Interior Castles* by St. Teresa of Avila. While her words were touching, I learned she started many convents and monasteries and eventually her own order. Why was she not considered a sixteenth-century feminist? How had the feminist movement become so secular? I had met so many grassroots women activists who derived power and strength from Christianity. For example, Maria Martinez of Latina Women for Choice told me, "When foundations refuse to fund our churches, our faith, they leave out our women."

As I thought about how closeted my faith had become in my feminist work, I began to feel parallels between that and other times I personally had been cut off from both power and myself. My Christian faith gives me an inner strength that fuels my hope and my determination. At the heart of Christianity is the image of Jesus on the cross. In the face of brokenness, humiliation, and pain, I can perceive an eventual triumph. With the image of Christ on the cross in my heart, hopelessness is not part of my vocabulary—it literally connects me to my empowerment. It *is* empowerment. Moreover, it informs my values. Jesus ushered in an "upside down kingdom," where walking with the powerless was the way to Godliness. He said, "Blessed are the poor, for yours is the kingdom of God." And, "Suffer the little children to come unto me, for such is the kingdom of God." The ministry of Jesus flips everything over.

And this is what feminists do, too. Feminist philanthropists put grantees on the boards. The abolitionist feminists made the African American women in their organization officers at the Convention, rather than exclusively white women. And their phrase "We're turning the world upside down" echoes the revolutionary teachings of Jesus Christ. Back in 1981, Swanee and I began doing joint philanthropy, but, as I recognized the need to create a bridge between faith and funding, I formed The Sister Fund and was joined by Reverend Kanyere Eaton, who currently pastors Fellowship Covenant Church in the Bronx. Our goal was to support and give voice to women working for justice within a faith-based framework. Explicitly stated, our mission was "Women transforming faith; faith transforming feminism."

Our grant making began to heal the dissonance between the faith-based community and feminism. We cofounded a global program, Faith, Feminism and Philanthropy, that introduced an arm of funding within the Women's Funding Network. The importance of giving faith a place at the table was often the major power that sustained and fueled grantees' activism. Slowly Kanyere and I were seeding a Christ- and faith-centered activism throughout the global network of women's funds.

It all started to integrate for me: Feminism is a revolutionary concept. Jesus was a revolutionary. I wanted to be clear to myself and those with whom I worked and interacted that it was my Christian faith that gave birth to my activism. The feminist revolution is so needed around the world, and God was telling me I had to speak out. This was not about my personal agenda. Within every fiber of my being, I knew I could not just enjoy my position of wealth and spend my time at the country club. I had a responsibility to do all I could to help the culture wake up using the significant resources I had. My activism was a vocation, an expression of my deepest soul. It was who God created me to be. To become overt about this, and work with Kanyere to unleash funding to faith-based feminism, was my assignment from God. Rather than abandon faith practices to those who would use them for the exact opposite of what they truly are, Kanyere and I and others sought a way to renew their promise.

Almost a decade later, when I discovered the early abolitionist women, I saw that I had been created just like them. They who spoke of their "holy duty" and preached so eloquently of the hand of God in their work. Their lives confirmed that I, too, could practice a feminism that invited me to bring all parts of myself forward—even my belief in God and love for Jesus. Nothing exiled, nothing inappropriate, nothing too taboo to discuss. I was following the blueprint of the earliest abolitionist feminists. To me, it was tragic that so many of the religious roots of feminism remained underground. Tender shoots were emerging. What might bloom if feminist Christianity was unleashed?

CHAPTER ONE

BAND OF SISTERS

Confusion has seized us, and all things go wrong,
The women have leaped from "their spheres,"
And instead of fixed stars, shoot as comets along,
And are setting the world by the ears!
. . . .
So freely they move in their chosen ellipse,
The "Lords of Creation" do fear an eclipse.

—MARIA WESTON CHAPMAN

It was October 21, 1835. Maria Weston Chapman felt the meeting hall tremble around her, rocked by the force of five thousand pairs of stomping feet on the cobblestone streets outside. Her face and voice betrayed no alarm as she surveyed the group of forty-five women who had come together for a meeting of the Boston Female Anti-Slavery Society. Their very presence had awakened a slumbering giant of protest. No other gathering of women had ever instigated such a vicious chorus of dissent. And no other female gathering had been so poised for a clash of morality, ideals, and identity.

This clash took place on the first-year anniversary of the formation of the Boston Female Anti-Slavery Society, started by twelve women in 1834.[1] Maria, a prominent socialite in the Boston community, was among its leaders, stepping outside the restricted bounds of her social status and gender to join the others.[2] Maria was not new to intellectual pursuits or to social action; founding the Boston Female Anti-Slavery Society was the culmination of a lifetime of learning and soul searching. She had been raised the eldest of six children in a Unitarian household in Weymouth, Massachusetts, and married a Unitarian who shared her abolitionist views. Her three unmarried sisters joined in her abolition work, devising a fundraising scheme in the form of "Anti-Slavery Fairs," which raised thousands of dollars for the cause. They sold a variety of goods for ladies, including aprons, cloaks, purses, quilts, and dolls, and, in spite of their subversive purpose, the fairs were very popular.

But as eagerly as the women embraced their mission, its public nature made it controversial. At the time, the cultural ideal for upper-class white women, known as the "cult of true womanhood," highlighted their moral superiority, but limited their influence to the domestic realm.[3] This "true womanhood" was expressed in four attributes: piety, purity, submissiveness, and domesticity. Piety in that a woman was the keeper of morality in her family and community, but was also subject to it, while men were permitted to be more profane. Purity meaning a woman was chaste, belonging only to her husband, and her sexuality completely dependent on him. Submissiveness required a woman to remain passive, obedient, and mostly silent about her beliefs and opinions. Domesticity in that a woman's purpose was the perfection of home life. Home and hearth was her realm, and there alone should she shine.

This cultural ideal was meant to effectively silence women on public matters, even as they were paid lip service as the moral core of the family and society. When these women began to speak out on the evils of slavery, a violent backlash rained down on them. In every instance of protest, they were chastised and reviled, whether from the pulpits of their own churches or the centers of commerce.

The founders of the Boston Female Anti-Slavery Society stirred controversy by associating with abolitionist firebrands such as William Lloyd Garrison. A young white man impassioned by the antislavery movement, Garrison had established a weekly periodical in 1830 as a megaphone for those voices calling for the immediate abolition of slavery. The *Liberator*'s masthead proclaimed, "Our country is the world—our countrymen are all mankind," an expression of universal oneness with a single consciousness most closely expressed as love.[4] In the early years, black men and women were the majority of subscribers to the paper and wrote approximately one-fifth of its articles. Garrison was refreshingly outspoken about the "potent" influence of women, and he did not hesitate to support their efforts, making him even more despised in establishment circles.[5]

Amid this fraught atmosphere, Maria Weston Chapman and her sisters strode onto the public stage. Although many vitriolic aspersions were cast against them, the abolitionist women of the Boston Female Anti-Slavery Society were strong, linking their cause with the gospel of Jesus Christ. As the first anniversary of their founding neared, they decided to hold an annual meeting and published an announcement in newspapers, asking that it be read in churches as well:

> By leave of Providence, the annual meeting of the Boston Female Anti-Slavery Society will be [held] on October 14, in Congress Hall, at 3 o'clock P.M. An address will be delivered by George Thompson. Ladies generally are invited to attend.

The response was rapid and furious. Newspapers and churches were full of declamation for the "undignified" women. One might speculate whether it was the involvement of George Thompson, a notorious British abolitionist, or the open invitation to ladies that created such a stir. It was widely believed that the women were not acting on their own—they could not possibly know their own minds in such serious matters! Plainly, they had been seduced by those wild abolitionist men. The belief in a woman's weak nature was so entrenched that people literally could not fathom that they had the presence of mind to act on their own. The ladies in question begged to differ, indignantly firing off a letter in the *Courier*:

> This association does firmly and respectfully declare that it is our right, and we will maintain it in Christian meekness, but with Christian constancy, to hold meetings, and to employ such lecturers as we judge best calculated

to advance the holy cause of human rights. . . . The cause of human freedom is our religion; the same taught us by him who died on Calvary—the great reformer, Christ. In it we will live—in it, if it must be so, we will die.[6]

The furor continued until finally the proprietors of Congress Hall announced that, in the interest of public safety, the ladies' society would not be allowed to hold its meeting there. Denied entry to Congress Hall, the women regrouped and announced that the meeting would be held on the afternoon of October 21 at the office of the *Liberator*.

Violence was openly threatened, and indeed, by early afternoon on the twenty-first, the throngs numbered some five thousand men—many loudly calling for the head of Thompson, although, unbeknownst to them, he was not in attendance after all. By 3:00 p.m., when the meeting was called to order, the mob outside was so fierce that the building shook. Crowds forced themselves inside and up the stairs, some hurling objects through the partition, while the women began their meeting with a reading from scripture. The women never became angry or cowered, but proceeded with a strong, serene focus on their business, as if immune to the frothing mob that seemed bent on doing them harm.

Suddenly, Theodore Lyman, the mayor of Boston, pushed his way into the meeting room, shouting, "Go home, ladies! Go home!" They stayed in place. Fearful of the mob outside, the mayor begged, "Ladies, do you wish to see a scene of bloodshed and confusion? If you do not, go home."

One of the women called out, "Mr. Lyman, your personal friends are instigators of this mob. Have you ever used your personal influence with them?"

"I know no personal friends," he protested. "I am merely an official. Indeed, ladies, you must retire. It is dangerous to remain."

At that point, a sense of calm came over Maria. She spoke in a firm voice that echoed above the roar below: "If this is the last bulwark of freedom, we may as well die here as anywhere."

Garrison, who knew that much of the rioters' anger was directed at him, decided to leave, hoping to take the angry mob with him. Some did follow him, threw a rope around him, and dragged him through the streets of Boston before Mayor Lyman stopped them and jailed Garrison for his own protection.

There was still a large, angry gathering outside as Maria finally rose to her feet and invited the women to retire to her home and continue their meeting.

They walked out of the building in a silent procession as the crowd slowly parted to let them through. They would later report that their hearts were broken as the faces of their tormenters came into focus. This mob was not rabble but comprised of some of the most upstanding members of the community. These were men they recognized as friends and neighbors—even some who privately had supported the abolition efforts. Maria saw members of her church and felt great sadness that the customary warmth had gone from their eyes and the smiles from their lips.

Later, when they learned that Garrison had been accosted by the mob, one of the women hesitantly asked if they should repent if their actions resulted in the deaths of friends and family. The women cried, "No!" They knew their cause was righteous, a manifestation of their Christian faith. They had to stand up for themselves, their beliefs, and their children. They would not relent.

THIS WAS NOT the first assault on these courageous ladies, nor would it be the last. The cause of the abolition of slavery, which drew them from their hearths, was a benchmark in an era of radical societal change.

In the early decades of the nineteenth century, America's soul was still bound up with slavery. The nation faced a shameful and divisive conflict; with the exponential growth of slavery in the South, the North and South were growing apart more each year. Attempting liberation of the slaves was a band of sisters, both black and white, whose weapons were courage, intelligence, faith, and solidarity. These women envisioned a new society where the full expression of democracy and Christian values would be denied to none. They did not speak out in a vacuum. The creation of ladies' antislavery societies was not an anomaly that occurred overnight or without social context. Rather, the times themselves had organized to make the women's new role a possibility.

Three significant cultural trends converged as a backdrop that allowed white women to find a voice and a cause in abolition: the Industrial Revolution, which changed the nature of work and family life; the influence of the Enlightenment, which created new expectations about human rights; and the Second Great Awakening, a populist religious movement that defined a more personal and accessible spiritual experience.

The Industrial Revolution began in the textile mills in northern England in the middle of the eighteenth century and soon spread to America. New technologies led to the creation of small factories manufacturing everyday products, such as cloth and shoes. Industrialization changed family structures as people shifted from agrarian to urban life. For the first time, men left home in large numbers for employment and the promise of upward mobility. Their wives were left in charge of the domestic arena, where the husbands had dominated. The new social guidelines directing women toward a cult of true womanhood gave them authority exclusively over the moral lives of their families. They had no social or political influence outside the home.

Industrialization delivered a separate, more ambiguous message to poorer women. They, too, went off to the factories, lured by the opportunity to make money. It was usually a false lure. Paid less than men, these women were deprived of the promise of economic opportunity and promotion.

Industrialization also enhanced the slave economy. By the 1830s, cotton was America's most lucrative export. The Southern states supplied the textile industry of New England with most of its raw material and purchased much of the grain, beef, and pork produced in the region referred to as the Old Northwest, such as Ohio and Pennsylvania. This economic interdependence gave Southern slaveholders significant influence in the North, and led to an increased reliance on slavery.

There was an upheaval growing beneath the surface of this new economy, for while many prospered, the gap between wealthy industrialists and working people grew cavernous. Street violence was not just aimed at the wealthy but also at free black people, who were seen as taking jobs from white workers. Racial tensions were exacerbated by economic strife, and women were in the middle, struggling for a foothold.

The social changes brought about by this economic flux were heightened by the philosophy of the Enlightenment. A European movement of the seventeenth and eighteenth centuries, the central theme of the Enlightenment was human progress through reason. This new intellectual framework promoted individual and natural rights and equality for all. The Enlightenment contributed to the French and American revolutions, with independence and self-reliance as central values.

Ironically, the originators of this enlightened ideology only meant their ideas to apply to a select group—affluent white men. They explicitly excluded people of color, landless men, and women. Many women read Enlightenment philosophy and found resonance in its tenets, but were frustrated that it was not meant for them. The very philosophy that elevated white men left their wives and daughters trapped in a lower realm.

As women and people of color chafed at their exclusion, they began to see that if they were to share in the new spirit of individual liberty and equality, they would have to mount another revolution—and they found the path in an awakening of faith.

At the time, a powerful wave of religious reformation

was sweeping across America. It was a time of tent revivals and the "democratization of religion." The Second Great Awakening ushered in a populist form of Christianity, attracting masses who believed Jesus dwells not within the church walls but within the individual. Previously, clergy interpreted the scripture; now people were reading it for themselves and felt called to create a kingdom of God here on earth. Many of the faithful saw their role as keeping the new materialism of industrialization in check. The leading evangelists preached a passionate relational theology, a stark contrast to the dogmatic hierarchical rules and everlasting punishment of early American Calvinism. Religious faith became deeply personal and less doctrinaire. New converts became reformers, taking seriously the message of the scriptures to do justice and love mercy. Large numbers of people opened their hearts to the indwelling (spiritual possession) of Jesus. Women in particular were drawn to this message because of their moral position in their households. They began bringing their husbands and male relatives to the revivals. The religious revival usurped some of the authority husbands previously held over their wives, giving women authority in the area of moral reform. With the revivalist movement, the emphasis was on change—starting a new, reformed life. And out of this sense of spiritual responsibility, some women became social reformers.

Transcendentalists, who were convinced that an ideal order "transcended" the concrete material world, also encouraged social reform. A prominent member of this circle, writer and intellectual Margaret Fuller, predicted that a new era would soon dawn for men *and* for women.[7]

Transcendentalism, along with a wide variety of faiths—Quakerism, spiritualism, premillennialism, Unitarianism, and Universalism—all stimulated feelings of spiritual intensity and social immediacy. This energy soon focused on the human stain of slavery.

RESISTANCE TO SLAVERY was as old as the practice itself, beginning when Africans leaped to their deaths from the decks of slave ships rather than embark on their hopeless journey. White opposition to slavery came later when members of the Quaker faith spoke out against the practice in the early 1700s. Other religious groups did not join the fight until the revivals "awakened" them to the notion that all people were God's children. But even these passionate protests were no match for the overwhelming economic engine that was dependent on slavery, and the explosive growth of the cotton industry increased the demand for slaves. White evangelical Christians and Spiritualists soon joined with African Americans and Quakers in the fight against slavery. When the North began to protest the expansion of slavery in the South, the South reacted defensively. Hostility increased. Verbal and political warfare ensued. In 1837 the country was perfectly divided—thirteen slave states and thirteen free states.

As the North and South sharpened their words and their weapons, one group of citizens decided repatriation was the answer. The founders of the American Colonization Society, some of whom were slaveholders and others passionately opposed to slavery, reasoned that if free black people were simply shipped to other parts of the world, the country would be free of the task of integration. David Walker, an ex-slave turned activist, helped to thwart the colonization movement. America was now the country of his people and he would fight to keep it that way. In 1829 Walker wrote *Appeal to the Colored Citizens of the World*, exhorting his brothers and sisters to claim their power, using violence if necessary.[8] His book "alarmed society not a little," according to British sociologist Harriet Martineau, and the Quaker abolitionist Benjamin Lundy called it the most inflammatory publication in history.[9] Georgia and North Carolina immediately enacted laws against "incendiary publications." Years later, Maria W. Stewart, an abolitionist author and speaker, called Mr. Walker "most noble, fearless, and undaunted," and asked, "Where is the man that has distinguished himself in these modern days by acting wholly in defense of African rights and liberty? There was one. Although he sleeps, his memory lives."[10]

Maria Stewart is believed to be the first American-born woman to write and deliver a political lecture. Unique for the time, she would also address integrated and mixed-gender audiences. She was primarily concerned with women's rights and social justice within the black community. Six years before white abolitionist feminists had begun to organize, Stewart was already calling for black women's financial independence and identity apart from that of wife and mother. An early adopter of the principles of relationality, she encouraged black women to use their commitment to one another to advocate for jobs and against discrimination. For Stewart the struggle wasn't just abolishing slavery, but something much more radical: for black people to become full and equal US citizens.

Maria Stewart delivered several public speeches, which encouraged both the black population as well as women of all races to claim their God-given equality. Her speeches challenged the treatment of the free black population in Northern cities, pointing out the hypocrisy embedded in abolitionist critiques of the South. Garrison published Stewart frequently in the *Liberator*, making her one of the earliest black female orators to have surviving copies of her lectures. William Lloyd Garrison published *Productions of Mrs. Maria W. Stewart*, a collection of four speeches delivered in Boston, and the book reached wide distribution.

Garrison was influenced by similar ideas made popular by Elizabeth Heyrick, a prominent Quaker and radical abolitionist in Britain. Heyrick's influence spread to the United States through an 1824 pamphlet, *Immediate Not Gradual Abolition*. In it, she wrote:

> The slave holder knew very well that his prey would be secure, so long as the abolitionists could be cajoled into a demand for gradual instead of immediate abolition. He knew very well that the contemplation of a gradual emancipation would beget a gradual indifference to emancipation itself.

William Lloyd Garrison's championing of radical equality inspired many white Christians to join the Quakers and people of color in the abolition fight. The abolitionists called on the country to live up to its creed of "liberty and justice for all," and for the church to practice the ideals of Christian love and unity it preached. Out of this ferment a small group of women came together, raising up their voices for freedom.

The new ideas of democracy and human dignity, with an emphasis on rights and freedom, fed the movements for abolition and women's rights. But the core of this movement was even more profound, because abolitionist feminists faced a nation and a church whose practices had become incongruent with both the laws of God and man. The Christian faith preached the sanctity of all life, even as slavery was sanctioned from the pulpits of its churches. The American ethic espoused freedom and justice for all, while it systematically enforced slavery and denied all women full legal status.

As women spiritually woke up, they took their interpretation of scripture to heart and were ready to act in new, bold ways. The systemic brutality of slavery shook their consciences. If they believed the words of Christ when he said God dwelled in each person's soul, and that Christianity called them to do unto others as they would have done to them, how could they tolerate such a system? As Maria W. Stewart so vividly put it in an 1831 address in Boston, "[I]t is not the color of the skin that makes the man or the woman, but the principle formed in the soul. Brilliant wit will shine, come from whence it will; and genius and talent will not hide the brightness of its lustre." The abolitionist feminists echoed the conviction that at their essence all share a universal humanity. Acting on this belief, the women broke through the prevailing social barriers. In sisterhood, they started a revolution, and they refused to listen to those who believed they had no right to join this fight.

"What if I am woman?" Stewart asked. "Is not the God of ancient times the God of these modern days? Did he not raise up Deborah, to be a mother and a judge in Israel? Did not Queen Esther save the lives of the Jews? And Mary Magdalene first declare the resurrection of Christ from the dead?"

LUCRETIA MOTT WAS only five feet tall, a white woman unassuming in her Quaker gray, but there was a strength in her manner that drew people to her. An outspoken abolitionist whose family home was a station on the Underground Railroad, she chafed at the Quaker custom of sitting in silence. Quaker practice was, however, light-years ahead of other religious denominations in allowing men and women equal place at meetings. Yet even this more enlightened religious group practiced racial discrimination, including relegating African American Quakers to a back bench. Increasingly, the dissonance between the practice of slavery and the moral imperative of freedom was intolerable. Lucretia's voice soon spread beyond the Friends meeting hall and she became influential in abolitionist circles. Lucretia urged her Quaker sisters to use their moral compass to express a new public authority. Out of that authority, they in turn developed a growing confidence in their own opinions and their ability to voice them.

Lucretia had a warm relationship with Garrison, whose respect for women's voices was well known. She first met him in 1830, when he was traveling through Philadelphia, having just been released from a seven-week prison term for slandering a slave owner. He had been told to meet Lucretia Mott and her husband James, and he made a point of it. Lucretia was impressed by Garrison's passion and wanted others to hear him. She secured a public meeting hall and invited everyone she knew to come and hear this inspiring man. But she was disappointed when he spoke. Not only did he simply read his speech, he mumbled it—unacceptable to Lucretia. He needed her coaching. She was blunt: "William, if thee expects to set forth thy cause by word of mouth, thee must lay aside thy paper and trust in the leading of the Spirit."[11] Despite her criticism—or perhaps because of it—they became lifelong friends. Soon after leaving this meeting, Garrison returned to Boston, bought a printing press, and published the first issue of the *Liberator*, which he mailed out on January 1, 1832.

Lucretia was enthusiastic when the American Anti-Slavery Society—founded by Garrison along with the Arthur Tappan—was formed in her hometown. (Famed activist Frederick Douglass often spoke at the meetings.) She was proud to be involved in planning the organization's founding convention in December 1833—one of four women among sixty-two men, representing ten of the free states. She secured the meeting place, arranged for refreshments, and over the course of the three days joined several other women in contributing to the discussion and wording of the constitution. At one point, she asked the chairman if she might speak, and was allowed to address the delegates.

The convention drafted the *Declaration of Sentiments and Purposes*, proclaiming that the moral ground had shifted beneath the institution of slavery. It was a heady moment. However, when the time came to sign their names to the *Declaration* as members, the women were not invited to sign.[12] If they had, they would have become de facto members of the organization, and it never occurred to the men to admit them. Sadder still, it didn't occur to the women to demand it.

One of the convention members, the minister Samuel J. May, described in his memoirs his later regret:

> It is one of the proudest recollections of my life that I was a member of the Convention in Philadelphia, in December, 1833, that formed the American Anti-Slavery Society. Nor shall I ever forget the wise, the impressive, the animating words spoken in our Convention by dear Lucretia Mott and two or three other excellent women who came to that meeting by divine appointment. But with this last recollection will be forever associated the mortifying fact, that we *men* were then so blind, so obtuse, that we did not recognize those women as members of our Convention, and insist upon them subscribing their names to our "Declaration of Sentiments and Purposes."[13]

So, here was the bitter reality that women could work on administrative tasks: send out notices, propose meals, and make all the arrangements for the meeting. They could even (rarely) speak, as Lucretia had. But when it came time to raise a hand to vote or sign, they were excluded. It was a moment of truth for Lucretia. She was not willing to be relegated to the sidelines; she decided that women must act on their own.

Three days later, Lucretia gathered a group of twenty-one women in the Philadelphia schoolroom of Catherine McDermott, a Quaker teacher, and there they formed the Philadelphia Female Anti-Slavery Society. The following week they finalized their constitution, stating, "We deem it our duty, as professing Christians, to manifest our abhorrence of the flagrant injustice and deep sin of slavery by united and vigorous exertions."

In time, the Philadelphia Female Anti-Slavery Society became the largest, most successful of the women's societies and a launching pad for women's political activism. It was a learning process for women unaccustomed to taking the reins. When Lucretia was asked to head this group, she recalled, "[A]t the time I had no idea of the meaning of preambles and resolutions and votings. Women had never been in any assemblies of this kind. I had only attended one Convention—a Convention of colored people in this State." She deferred the responsibility of chairing the first meeting to a black male friend, the minister James McCrummill. She later made this wry observation about his participation: "You know that at that time, even to the present day, Negroes, idiots, and women were in legal documents classed together; so that we were very glad to get one of our own class to come and aid in forming that society."[14]

But Lucretia did not defer long. Within this society she rose as a leading figure in the abolitionist movement and later in the struggle for women's rights. She always defended women's right to speak, and this diminutive woman in Quaker gray became a giant in capability and vision. She had the power, as abolitionist orator Wendell Phillips once remarked, to correct critics with "a silken snapper on her whiplash." The question for Lucretia was not so much whether women and men were equal; rather, it was how to remove the barriers so the full spirit of women could be liberated for the good of all.

The Philadelphia Female Anti-Slavery Society further distinguished itself by being interracial from the start. In defiance not only of social restrictions but in stark contrast to male abolition societies, at least nine of the society's early members were black.[15] One of the founding members was Amy Hester "Hetty" Reckless, a runaway slave from New Jersey. Reckless was introduced to the feminist abolitionist circle by the Quaker family she was living with at the time. Reckless operated a station on the Underground Railroad, and in 1838 worked with the majority-black Vigilant Association of Philadelphia, first with its female branch and later as a member of the board. With funding help from the Philadelphia Female Anti-Slavery Society, the Vigilant Association saved the lives of thirty-five runaway slaves. In later years Hetty Reckless would continue to work with Sarah Mapps Douglass to educate and provide job skills to black women, widening their means of livelihood.

The abolitionist women had an innate sense of sophistication in their political organizing. The goal was social activism "with" not "for" black people—a radical interracial egalitarianism. They wanted to acknowledge their new ethic by embodying it. They took to heart the words written decades earlier by Phillis Wheatley, a poet and the first published black woman in America: "In every human breast, God has implanted a Principle, which we call love of freedom."[16] Wheatley's words had inspired black women to step forward against the deep racism and sexism in American culture, and were doing so again as a female-led abolitionist movement began to take shape.

A spark had set fire to the female conscience across the North. Facing riots, threats, and blasphemy, ladies' antislavery societies began to proliferate. In 1833 there were seven female antislavery societies; in 1834 seventeen new societies emerged; in 1835 twenty-nine more were formed; in 1836 forty-two; and in 1837 forty-five. By the end of 1837 there would be nearly 140 societies, creating a large network of abolitionist feminists. Some societies were black, others white, and others integrated.

There were many distinctions among local societies, but they drew on a common inspiration—"sympathy for the slave"—which became their rallying cry.[17] How could their neighbors continue to buy cotton goods and use cane sugar without facing the destructive effect this had on black families in the South? (Women were the buyers in their families, and some of them were now introducing the radical idea that what is purchased could be a political and moral statement.) In prayer and study of the scriptures, they found the holy blueprint for their cause—a God-ordained duty to speak out on behalf of the enslaved. Their sense of religious calling began to confound accepted Christian principles. The institutional church went on record saying that women who spoke publicly were unsexing themselves and violating New Testament doctrine. Yet in their hearts, the women knew this was false.

By claiming "sympathy," they were not speaking of pity or condescension. In this context and era, sympathy referred to developing a new awareness—intentionally practicing a new set of feelings for the slaves. But their practice was much more like what is commonly called "empathy" today—that is, the practice of respectfully seeking to learn about and participate in the feelings of another. For them, the best way to understand the real human cost of slavery was to attempt to feel it in their own bodies. They urged mothers to imagine how they would feel if they were separated from their husbands, or their children were taken away; to imagine the suffering of the slaves as though it was their own. These abolitionist women encouraged people to think of the slaves as human beings with the same feelings—and even the same blood—as themselves. The Sermon on the Mount, Christ's revolutionary message, was their model, with its charter of ethics and the Golden Rule.

In the midst of this radical social revisioning, another tension was emerging. Not only were women questioning the hypocrisy of the political system, they were also rejecting certain established church doctrines. Organized religion supported slavery *and* was one of the most formidable foes of women's rights. The women challenged this dual bigotry, laying claim to the higher good of humanity. In July 1836, addressing the women of Massachusetts at the Boston Female Anti-Slavery Society, Maria Weston Chapman spoke to those who would cloak their support of slavery in religion:

As immortal souls, created by God to know and love him with all our hearts, and our neighbor as ourselves, we owe immediate obedience to his commands, respecting the sinful system of Slavery, beneath which 2,500,000 of our Fellow-Immortals, children of the same country, are crushed, soul and body, in the extremity of degradation and agony.

As women, it is incumbent upon us, instantly and always, to labor to increase the knowledge and the love of God that such concentrated hatred of his character and laws may no longer be so entrenched in men's business and bosoms, that they dare not condemn and renounce it. . . .

Let but each woman in the land do a Christian woman's duty, and the result cannot fail to be [the slave's] instant, peaceful, unconditional deliverance. Thus, and thus only can we hope to deliver our own souls. Only in thus doing, can we hope to hear the voice of Jesus, saying unto us, "Come, ye blessed of my Father!—Inasmuch as ye have done it unto the least of these my brethren, ye have done it unto me!"[18]

QUAKER WOMEN, SUCH as Lucretia Mott, encouraged women to take aim at the evils of slavery. It is interesting to note, however, that religious diversity was an emblem of this special movement. Mary Grew was only twenty years old when the Philadelphia Female Anti-Slavery Society was founded, yet as the devout daughter of a Baptist minister, she felt called to the message of faith and action embodied in its purpose.

Mary had been raised in Connecticut and studied at the Hartford Female Seminary, founded by Catharine

Beecher (educator and sister of Harriet Beecher Stowe, author of *Uncle Tom's Cabin*), one of the best schools in the country for young women. Mary's father, Henry, supported education for girls and gave money to the school. Both Catharine Beecher and Henry Grew helped nurture Mary's growth. Armed with an inner confidence developed under their mentorship, Mary became an advocate for a radical idea that neither one of them could fully support—equality for women.

In the early 1830s, the Grew family moved to Philadelphia. There, Mary and her half sister Susan were early members of the Philadelphia Ladies' Anti-Slavery Society. In November 1834, the society opened a school for black children, which Mary was asked to organize and oversee. By the next year, the school had twenty-seven students. And in 1836, she became the society's corresponding secretary, a role she embraced with fervor—and which she would serve for over three decades. She wrote the annual reports and one day had the impulse to send them to other societies, which began the process of knitting together the disparate organizations into a collaborative whole.

Impressed by the emerging sisterhood, Maria Weston Chapman, who was corresponding secretary for the Boston society, wrote to Mary in 1836 with a proposal: a national meeting that would bring together women from antislavery societies across the North. She suggested that they join forces, uniting the female societies in one voice to appeal to Congress for greater justice. Mary agreed that petition drives were a way for women to speak out against slavery and that the convention would be a means to launch a national campaign. She wrote that Maria's idea was "expedient and desirable," and suggested that the meeting be held the following May in New York City. The two women set out to spread the word, and they invited the women's societies to elect delegates.

Grew encouraged the legal societies to send delegates to New York City for the convention as well. Word spread. And societies began to sign on to help organize the first national women's conference in the United States, the Anti-Slavery Convention of American Women of 1837, which would take place from May 9 to 12. Maria recorded their progress:

> We have received from friends in all parts of the country copious lists of the names of such Ladies as are by zeal & experience qualified to carry into execution any judicious ideas, and what we propose to do is . . . [encourage] A Meeting of Ladies . . . to meet—to talk—to pray together—to compare feelings & opinions; to see on earth the faces of those beloved fellow-labouress. . . . These are the soul of the enterprise.[19]

Articulating the "soul of the enterprise"—collaboration in prayer and action—ignited new energy and vision. A flurry of letters followed, and soon the women were discussing strategy for a national campaign against slavery. Their vision moved from local action to winning converts for abolition to a much bolder plan—one that would require them to lay claim to their right to speak out and assert leadership as women. Their mission was too important to wait for society to grant them permission.

At the time of the planning, the women could not

have known that their 1837 convention would become a signaling event for women in public life. They only knew that sharing support and ideas among their sisterhood was something they must do, against all odds. They drew strength from each other across the miles and rejoiced that soon they would meet their abolitionist sisters face-to-face.

CHAPTER TWO

A CONVENTION LIKE NO OTHER

*I started up, and with one mighty effort threw
from me the lethargy which had covered me as a
mantle for years; and determined, by the help of
the Almighty, to use every exertion in my power
to elevate the character of my wronged and
neglected race.*

—SARAH MAPPS DOUGLASS

May 1837. The women came. Defying a myriad of social constraints and against all odds they came. Traveling by stagecoach and steamboat, they arrived in New York City, breathless and expectant, to convene the first Anti-Slavery Convention of American Women. They left their sanctioned roles to step out into the world. Emboldened by the greatness of the cause and the strength of their sisterhood, they chose to raise a loud cry against the greatest moral evil of the times. For this, they were mocked and censured, but still they came, vowing to proclaim a vision for a new era. And take the first steps of action.

Denied permission to gather from the male antislavery establishment, they relied on an inalienable authority from God. "You are the light of the world," proclaimed the gospel. And they became that light. These courageous women, numbering some two hundred, set aside family obligations, conspired to raise funds in the midst of an economic depression, and did what was necessary to take their God-granted part in catalyzing the cultural upheaval necessary for this moment in history.

The convention was scheduled for May 9–12, 1837, at the Third Free Church, located on the corner of Houston and Thompson—in today's Greenwich Village.[1] The location could easily accommodate their numbers—it had seating for eighteen hundred—but it also reflected their egalitarian ethic. It was called a "free church" because the pews were not auctioned to wealthy church members. The women had worked for months planning, with many societies exchanging minutes and reading them at their meetings, which helped to fuel their imaginations and commitment to making their convention a reality.

These women on the cusp of making history represented at least twenty antislavery societies across ten states and almost four dozen towns. They were from all walks of life—aristocrat to laborer to former slave. They were of mixed Christian backgrounds—Quaker, Baptist, and Spiritualist. Most notably, in a first for antislavery gatherings, they were multiracial—black, white, and Native American. Many of the women were from small towns and, traveling unchaperoned to New York City, with its population of three hundred thousand, was in itself a daunting undertaking. None of them had ever participated in an event like this.

In spite of the women's diverse roots, their common mission was moral, intellectual, and deeply personal. They drew courage from each other and from their faith. The bonds of their sisterhood had been formed in a shared passion for justice, across states and communities, from cities, towns, and villages throughout the Northeast. Although most of them had never met face-to-face, they were soon to become as intimate as sisters.

Their diaries and letters recorded awe and excitement. One attendee described her astonishment at being there in a letter published in the *Liberator* in June 1837:

> On the morning of the 9th, after a pleasant ride of seventeen hours from Boston, I found myself in the 'London of America,' and for what? To attend a female convention! Once, I should have blushed at the thought, and exclaimed, prophecy it not in the streets of America that her daughters will ever thus pass the circumference of their accustomed sphere.

She went on to compare their convention to the Continental Congress:

> But now, I esteemed it a higher honor to be found in such an assembly than was enjoyed by those of our fathers who held a seat in the continental Congress when the immortal declaration was sent forth to the world. It is indeed a holier struggle for liberty now than then.

Free black women had been organizing in their communities before the female antislavery societies were formed. They had their own societies, such as the Colored Ladies Literary Society and the Rising Daughters of Abyssinia. What had begun as a benevolent effort to help the poor and sick in their midst turned more radical as slave-catchers roamed the North, sweeping up suspected escaped slaves for return to the South. In some cases, free black women fought slave-catchers, physically wresting their prey from them, and even breaking into jails, freeing escaped slaves and spiriting them away. A few joined female antislavery societies, where their presence wasn't always embraced. It is notable that the convention achieved a level of black participation that was more than three times greater than the percentage of black women in the entire free female population. One in ten of the convention-goers were black.

To reach the convention, some black and white women traveled together, making for a potentially dangerous journey. William Lloyd Garrison captured the interracial tension of the trip when he wrote to his wife of the experience of traveling with the abolitionist Julia Williams:

> Found several abolition friends in the car at the boat dock. . . . Took Julia Williams in with us . . . but expected she would be ordered out, as some of the passengers and bystanders cast certain significant glances at each other. [T]hey probably supposed . . . that she was our servant. . . . Ushered the ladies, Miss Julia included, into the Ladies' Cabin. . . . Had Miss Williams gone down to tea last evening . . . no doubt a great commotion would

have been stirred up—to prevent which . . . we had tea and breakfast brought up to her.[2]

Her companions knew that Williams's eating and sharing sleeping quarters with white passengers would generate hostility. But her presence among them was the reason they were convening. Their goal was to express—not just in words, but in actions—their commitment to the new social ethic of equality. In the *New Hampshire Herald of Freedom*, one white woman wrote,

> I was happy, in the early stages of this journey, to have our feelings tested with regard to that bitter prejudice against color, which we have so criminally indulged, and to find it giving place to better feelings. . . . [O]ur colored companion slept near my side—she rode with us in the carriage—sat with us at the table of a public boarding-house—walked in company with us.

The black representatives still had to brace themselves for the overt racism they knew to expect from some of the white convention attendees. For this reason, although the Colored Ladies Literary Society and the Rising Daughters of Abyssinia sent delegates, many other black women's societies did not. It was a bitter reality that, although the members of antislavery societies shared a common purpose to end slavery, they were not united in their embrace of black people as equals. Some of the white abolitionists objected to integration. For them the issue was clear cut: end slavery and its torments. But they were unwilling to take the next step, which was to consider black people as fully human.

For others, interracial organizing in the abolitionist societies was fundamental to the cause—and it caused a torrent of public backlash. For example, the Boston Female Anti-Slavery Society's minutes noted that the city's response to their interracial membership was to call the abolitionist women "mad." But the women were heartened by the fact that the disciple Paul had been considered mad as well, as he wrote in the book of Acts. They took courage from his response to the Roman governor Festus, who had once declared, "Paul, you are out of your mind! Your great learning is driving you mad." To which he replied, "I am not out of my mind, most excellent Festus, but I utter words of sober truth."

Racist sentiment was particularly high within the Ladies' New York City Anti-Slavery Society. In particular, its leader, Abigail Ann Cox, was quite vocal about the fact that black women were not welcome to join the New York Society. Disgusted by this, Anne Warren Weston of the Boston Society wrote to her sister, Deborah, "Mrs. Cox is the life and soul of the New York Society and she is in a very sinful state—full of wicked prejudice about colour; they do not allow any coloured women to join their society."[3] (The Ladies' New York City Anti-Slavery Society, which was integrated at its inception, eventually became exclusively white.)

Anticipating prejudice at the convention, one of the organizers, Angelina Grimké, wrote to a friend:

> Now it does seem to us that we had better have no National Society until we can have one of the right stamp, & I do not think one can flourish in this city while

Prejudice banishes our colored sisters from an equal & full participation in its deliberations & labors. I am greatly in hopes that the Boston Society will send colored Delegates to the Convention.[4]

By "the right stamp," Angelina meant giving a place at the table to the women most impacted by the issue being discussed. This early conflict would not be easily resolved, as it reflected a racial standoff that still existed in the larger antislavery community. But in the end, inclusion became a signature element of the abolitionist feminists' blueprint.

At last reaching New York City, the travelers drew their first breath of the pungent urban air and felt the electric pulse of commerce as they made their way down rough, narrow streets to the Third Free Church. Some first attended the opening meeting of the American Anti-Slavery Society Convention at the Broadway Tabernacle on the morning of May 9, which preceded their meeting. Their presence as mere bystanders at the all-male meeting highlighted the purpose of their own convention: at last, a place where they could speak, collaborate, and be heard. When the meeting ended at 3:00 p.m., the women rose and marched down the cobblestone streets to the Third Free Church to meet their sisters.

Slowly the high-backed pews began to fill. The Quakers were in full force, in their dark gray suits and simple white caps. Other women, such as those from the New York City Ladies' Anti-Slavery Society, were in brighter dresses with shawls, an occasional ruffle, and matching bonnets. All looked determined as they took their seats and waited for their convention to begin. Certainly, the structure of their gathering was similar to the male abolitionist meetings, but this was no imitation of the men's process; they had their own ideas and their own strategy. One female abolitionist wrote: "[W]e often hear that a female convention is . . . an unprecedented thing. True, but these are times without a precedent, and they call for new and peculiar action from every moral being in our land."[5]

ANGELINA GRIMKÉ LOOKED on, the thrill of the event coursing through her. It had been a long journey to reach this moment. Tall and graceful, with large expressive blue eyes and dark curls peaking out from under her Quaker cap, Angelina, along with her older sister, Sarah, had become among the most dependable members of the movement.

At thirty-three, Angelina was blessed with a striking charisma, unusual for the women of her time. Sarah, though quieter, was no less committed. The sisters possessed a unique insight as a result of having been raised in a prominent South Carolina slaveholding family. There they witnessed firsthand the plight of the family's slaves. Their experience festered in their consciences—as Sarah would say, "until they became like a canker, incessantly gnawing."[6]

Angelina had always looked up to Sarah, who at forty-six was thirteen years her senior. When they were children, Sarah had taken on a parental role with Angelina, to the extent that she still referred to her fondly as "Mother." Sarah became Angelina's mentor and role model, and her influence was most deeply felt in her convictions about the evils of slavery.

In spite of the overwhelming force of social custom, Sarah had instinctively hated slavery, even as a small child. Her earliest memory was of the revulsion she felt at the age of five when she saw a slave woman being beaten. Although her parents' Episcopalian church endorsed slavery, she was drawn to the scriptures' message of love for all, regardless of skin color. Her young mind was tormented by the irreconcilable conflict between the tenets of her faith and the actions of her church. Jesus taught love, and Paul preached equality, writing in his epistle to the Galatians, "There is neither Jew nor Greek, there is neither slave nor free, there is no male and female, for you are all one in Christ Jesus." She was distraught by the hypocrisy of God's representatives who could stand at the pulpit and declare, on one hand, the loving message of Christ and, on the other, the enslavement of a race of people.

Defying her father, Sarah taught Hetty, a slave girl in her household, to read. Sarah would later write, "I took an almost malicious satisfaction in teaching my little waiting-maid at night. . . . The light was put out, the keyhole screened, and flat on our stomachs before the fire, with the spelling-book under our eyes, we defied the law of South Carolina." They were caught and her father punished them both.[7]

Angelina, influenced by her sister, also rejected slavery at an early age. Eyes open, she pursued her sister's path and shared her penchant for theological probing.

The first to break from the family, Sarah moved to

Philadelphia in 1821. She had visited the city before, accompanying her father for medical care when he was ill. During the months they spent there, she gravitated away from the Episcopalian church to Quakerism. She also experienced a community without slavery for the first time. Months later, she made a permanent move. Angelina was disappointed that her sister left her at home with their mother, a strong advocate of slavery. But Sarah told Angelina how she had been inspired by stories of Joan of Arc, whose relationship with God was to her "the most remarkable exhibition of communication between God and man, Jesus excepted, that stands on the records of history." Impressed by the Quaker practice that gave women the same right as men to speak at meetings, Sarah found a spiritual home at the Fourth and Arch Street Meeting House of Friends. She wrote to Angelina, encouraging her to come and explore the Quaker tradition. In 1829, growing tired of the conflicts with her mother, Angelina finally joined Sarah, breaking free of the South. A friend later described the sisters as "voluntary exiles from the blood-stained soil of Carolina."[8]

In time, Angelina, with her spirited personality and talent for speaking, took the lead in abolition work as Sarah held back. Although Sarah was unwavering in her belief that slavery was wrong, and engrossed in the cause, she was hesitant about acting publicly. Angelina, however, was compelled to action, saying, "I desire to *talk* but little about religion, for words are empty sounds, but may my life be a living epistle known and read of all men."[9]

Early in 1835, Angelina began to attend meetings of the Philadelphia Female Anti-Slavery Society, where she joined the committee for the improvement of the people of color. Her breakout moment came after she read an editorial by William Lloyd Garrison in the *Liberator*. The piece, titled "Reign of Terror," detailed a mob attack on the Charleston, South Carolina, post office where antislavery materials had been sent for circulation in the South. The materials were destroyed. Angelina was so heartsick and outraged that she wrote a letter to Garrison, vowing to fight: "LET IT COME; for it is my deep, solemn, deliberate conviction, that *this is a cause worth dying for.*"

Without Angelina's knowledge, Garrison printed her letter in the *Liberator*. Overnight, Angelina became a public figure among abolitionists. One reader responded to her letter, saying she was "a stronger thinker than the leading pro-slavery lecturers."[10]

Increasingly, the sisters found themselves champing at the restrictions they felt even within the Friends community. Their initial attraction to the faith had been its virtuous embrace of abolition, which was a refreshing contrast to the hypocrisy of most religious traditions. However, as women, they had to fight to find a voice. Angelina wrote to her sister about her disillusionment with the Friends:

> The door of usefulness in our Society seems as if it was bar'd and double lock'd to me. I feel no openness among Friends; my spirit is oppressed and heavy laden and shut up in prison.[11]

The poet and abolitionist John Greenleaf Whittier found Sarah "serious, solemn—as if her heart lingered amidst the crushed and sorrowful tenants of the slave cabins of Carolina." Out of this despair and loneliness, Sarah and Angelina began to agitate in ways that would galvanize abolitionists nationwide.

Both of them turned to writing, releasing their pain and passion through words on paper. In May 1836, Angelina wrote her first book, *An Appeal to the Christian Women of the South*, which she completed in just two weeks. About the writing, she said, "It has all come to me; God has shown me what I can do." Angelina's *Appeal* was a cogent theological treatise. She drew from the scriptures to make her case against slavery, point by point. Its publication had a great impact in abolitionist circles in the Northeast—though not for its intended audience in her home state. South Carolinians never had a chance to read it. Copies sent to South Carolina were burned by the postmaster. When public officials learned that Angelina was planning to visit her mother and sisters in Charleston, the mayor himself went to see her mother and told her that police would not allow her daughter's steamer to land, and that if she stepped foot in the city she would be arrested. Angelina's Charleston friends warned her against coming, fearing violence against her and her family. Saddened, Angelina was persuaded to remain in the North.

Quieter, but determined, Sarah also took up her pen, writing letters to newspapers, which she published in her first pamphlet, *An Epistle to the Clergy of the Southern States*. In it, she declared that the Bible had been falsely translated by men; men and women were created equal; and they had equal responsibilities and rights, including the responsibility and right to speak out against slavery.

Basing these points on scripture enabled Sarah to address head-on one of the greatest opponents of women's rights—institutionalized religion. She attacked her critics on their own ground. The sisters' books created a firestorm, especially as they were the first women to write from the experience of growing up on a wealthy plantation with hundreds of slaves. Their childhood experiences afforded them the credibility to speak. For them the plight of slaves was not an abstraction; it was a living, breathing reality that they had witnessed on a daily basis. Their early shame was transformed into a sense of purpose.

Angelina was consumed with the idea that the biblical role of women gave them a special moral authority. Time and again in the scriptures, it was a woman who stood tall and defeated the forces of evil. The Old Testament was full of courageous women, such as Esther, Ruth, and Deborah, and there were strong women in the New Testament as well. As she wrote:

> There are Marys sitting in the house now, who are ready to arise and go forth in this work as soon as the message is brought, "the master is come and calleth for thee." And there are Marthas, too, who have already gone out to meet Jesus, as he bends his footsteps to their brother's grave, and weeps, not over the lifeless body of Lazarus bound hand and foot in grave-clothes, but over the politically and intellectually lifeless slave, bound hand and foot in the iron chains of oppression and ignorance.[13]

Now sitting in the great hall of the Third Free Church, listening to the excited roar of the conversations among women, Angelina and Sarah felt the loneliness of the past years dissolve.

THE GRIMKÉ SISTERS' hearts lifted as they looked across the convention hall and saw Grace and Sarah Mapps Douglass, their dear Quaker friends from Philadelphia—a mother and daughter who had labored valiantly for abolition. Grace Douglass had been born into a prominent, free multiracial family. She was one of the founding members of the Philadelphia Female Anti-Slavery Society and a leading educator for the black population. Her daughter followed in her footsteps.

Grace was the fifth of eight children born to Cyrus Bustill, a baker and son of a slave, and Elizabeth Morey Bustill, the daughter of an Englishman and a Delaware Native American woman. As a child, Grace attended a school for black children in Philadelphia. It was necessary in the free black community for both women and men to work to support their families, so it was natural for Grace to learn a trade. She took up millinery and opened a bonnet shop in her father's bakery. There she caught the eye of Robert Douglass, the barber who owned the shop next door. They married and over the years had six children. Considered part of Philadelphia's black elite, Grace and Robert were influential in the abolitionist community. Robert established the African Presbyterian Church of Philadelphia and was a minister there. European abolitionists would make the Douglass home a stopping point when visiting Philadelphia.

By the 1800s, Philadelphia had become the "city of hope" for black people in America. Pennsylvania was the first state to pass a gradual abolition act, which provided that children born of slaves be freed at the age of twenty-eight. Black people could find paid work as day laborers, domestic servants, and as mariners at the city's bustling port. Other free blacks, like Grace's father, started their own businesses, serving the growing black community. By 1830 14,500 of the total 150,000 people who lived in the city were freedmen and freedwomen—nearly ten percent.

Grace believed that to achieve more security and stability, her children had to have the best education possible. In that spirit, she and Robert enrolled their eldest daughter, Elizabeth, in an all-white school. Elizabeth excelled, outperforming her classmates. However, the white community began to resent Elizabeth's presence, and eventually the school asked her to leave. For two parents who wanted a high-quality education for their children, the experience was crushing. But Grace and Robert were determined to ensure their children's future and opened their own school for black children. Tragically, Elizabeth's health failed and she died at fifteen, the same year her parents opened their school.

The loss of her daughter and of two other children threatened to break Grace's heart in two. In despair, she found solace in her Christian faith. Recognizing the depth of Jesus's suffering and His ability to transcend it, she determined to follow His path. In the midst of tragedy, Grace experienced a spiritual transformation that gave her life new purpose. Fortified by prayer, Grace channeled her energies into social action. She described her experience in a letter to a local minister:

When I was first married . . . [w]e had our parties and tea-drinkings; we must have the best wine and the best cake; our friends had it and we must give them the same. . . . But when it pleased the Lord to open my eyes, these things became a burden to me. . . . When I became more engaged to follow Christ I remembered that when on earth, he went about doing good.

In 1832 she explained in the *Liberator* how thinking about Christ's example moved her into action:

I thought I would assist the poor too if I had the means some people had, but I have no more than I want myself; how can I help the poor? Then it occurred to me. . . . Now a pair of morocco shoes cost one dollar and 50 cts.: a pair of leather will do just as well, and I shall have 50 cts. for the poor. A fine muslin dress costs five dollars: I can buy a very good calico one for three, and have two dollars to spare.

During this period Grace and her daughter Sarah developed an especially close bond, and they were united in a process of personal enlightenment. They both believed that education was the key to equality and a good life for black children. In addition, the relationships that Grace and Sarah formed with white abolitionists increased the potential for empathy and openhearted engagement across races.

Before the 1830s, Grace and Sarah believed they contributed to racial equality simply by being upright members of the community. But in 1832, when Congress introduced a bill requiring all free black people to carry valid identification papers, they began to sense how vulnerable their whole race was, whether free or not, and they began to support the radical forces of abolition. Again in the *Liberator*, Sarah wrote,

> One short year ago, how different were my feelings on the subject of slavery! . . . I had formed a little world of my own, and cared not to move beyond its precincts. But how was the scene changed when I beheld the oppressor lurking on the border of my own peaceful home! I saw his iron hand stretched forth to seize me as his prey, and the cause of the slave became my own. I started up, and with one mighty effort threw from me the lethargy which had covered me as a mantle for years; and determined, by the help of the Almighty, to use every exertion in my power to elevate the character of my wronged and neglected race.

Together, Sarah and Grace organized other women to become antislavery activists. In 1831 Sarah helped found the Female Literary Association, a group formed to empower black women. The purpose of the association was for women to "feed our never-dying minds, to excite each other to deeds of mercy, words of peace; to stir up in the bosom of each, gratitude to God for his increasing goodness, and feeling of deep sympathy for our brethren and sisters, who are in this land of Christian light and liberty held in bondage the most cruel and degrading—to make their cause our own!" As an officer, Sarah insisted that the association focus on abolition. She said, "It is my wish that the reading and conversation should be altogether directed to the subject of slavery."[14]

In 1833, when Lucretia Mott called for the formation of a ladies' antislavery society, both the Grimkés and the Douglasses joined the cause and were committed to interracial organizing. Of the twenty-nine signers of the organization's constitution, at least nine, but possibly twelve, were black. (There is historical unclarity about the exact number.) In its second year, sixty-nine new members signed the constitution, nine of whom were black. Both Grace and Sarah provided years of leadership as officers, librarians, and workers for the fundraising fairs. As black women, they offered a crucial perspective that deepened the society's wisdom and effectiveness.

The Grimké sisters credited Grace and Sarah with opening their eyes to both the organizing potential of the black population and the discrimination that Northern black people faced. Over the years, the four women developed a warm friendship. Sarah Douglass and the Grimkés shared their deepest thoughts and feelings in an active exchange of letters that spanned forty years. Their relationship was remarkable in both its closeness and openness at a time when white and black people hardly ever spoke.

Their correspondence reveals how the Grimkés and the Douglasses agonized over the degradation of African Americans. Sarah and Angelina Grimké encouraged the Douglasses to continue attending abolition meetings, at the same time admitting that, of all the women in attendance, they—and the other black women abolitionists— were paying the highest cost.

Racism existed among the broad-minded Quakers, too. Black congregants were forced to sit on a reserved bench at the back of the room during meetings. Writing in 1837, Sarah Douglass described the prejudice her mother faced when she wanted to apply for Quaker membership:

> [My mother] mentioned her concern to a Friend who said do not apply, you will only have your feelings wounded. Friends will not receive you. Thus admonished, and feeling that prejudice had closed the doors against her, she did not make her concern known to the Society. There was nothing but my Mother's complexion in the way to prevent her being a member, she was highly intelligent & pious; her whole life blameless.

When asked about the Quaker Arch Street Meeting in particular, Sarah shared several more descriptions of "galling remonstrance," concluding, "I believe they despise us for our color." Sarah was deeply hurt when, as a teacher in New York, she attended a meeting and was approached by a white woman seeking "help."

> I had been attending meeting one month when a Friend accosted me thus, "Does thee go out ahouse cleaning." I looked at her with astonishment, my eyes filled with tears & I answered no. . . . Judge what were my feelings, a stranger in a strange land, think of the time, the place & this the first salutation I received in a house consecrated to Him. I wept during the whole of that mtg. & for many succeeding Sabbaths.[15]

Against this backdrop it is not surprising that Grace and Sarah were reluctant to attend the 1837 convention.

In addition to their troubling experiences in Philadelphia, they had heard stories about racism in the New York City Anti-Slavery Society. Black and white abolitionists, it seemed, often had different agendas. Both wanted slaves to be freed, but black people were more concerned with the broader issues of civil liberties. Many white abolitionists did not even pretend to share these goals.

The Grimkés urged them on and demanded that the Anti-Slavery Convention of American Women be racially integrated. They saw black women as their sisters in the struggle. Sarah Grimké wrote in a letter to Sarah Douglass, "I feel deeply for thee in thy suffering on account of the cruel and un-Christian prejudice which thou has suffered so much from. . . . The more I mingle with [black people], the more I feel their oppression & desire to sympathize with their sorrows."[16]

Persuaded by the Grimkés and knowing it was the right thing to do, the Douglasses set aside their concerns and decided to go to the convention. Once in New York, however, Grace suffered humiliation at a Quaker meeting. Her daughter Sarah recorded what happened:

> Mother does not recollect distinctly the circumstances that occurred at the New York Mtg. but thinks this is the substance. After she had been in Mtg. sometime a Friend came in & sat by her, & asked her who she lived with. Mother said she did not live with any one. The Fd. then said that the colored people sat up stairs "as Fds. do not like to sit by thy color."

In contrast, the Grimkés stayed constant in their support

of the dignity and wise leadership of the Douglasses. Sarah Douglass wrote,

> Did all the members of the Friends society feel for us, as the sisters Grimké do, how soon, how very soon would the fetters be stricken from the captive and cruel prejudice be driven from the bosoms of the professed followers of Christ. . . . [T]hey identified themselves with us, took our wrongs upon them, and made our oppression and woe theirs.[17]

Sarah records in several letters that the Grimkés sat with them in the "Negro seat" at Quaker meetings as a sign of their solidarity. The Grimké sisters credited the Douglasses with helping them understand that colonization—deporting free African Americans to colonies in Africa—was actually proslavery.

Thanks in large part to the strong convictions of the Grimkés and the courage of the Douglasses, the Anti-Slavery Convention of American Women in 1837 was the first significant interracial gathering in the country. The black poet Sarah Forten wrote the lines printed on the covers of most convention materials:

> We are thy sisters,—God has truly said,
> That of one blood, the nations he has made.
> O, Christian woman, in a Christian land,
> Canst thou unblushing read this great command?
> Suffer the wrongs which wring our inmost heart,
> To draw one throb of pity on thy part!

Our "skins may differ," but from thee we claim
A sister's privilege, in a sister's name.[18]

Forten invited all women to look beyond skin color and reflect on the "one blood" underneath, a deeper place where our common humanity resides. The language and leanings of "our inmost heart" would accomplish this. The call Forten made was for a relationship that she knew held vast power to heal.

AT FOUR O'CLOCK on the afternoon of May 9, 1837, a small white woman in Quaker attire stepped up to the podium. The room quieted. Lucretia Mott began her remarks with a deliberate tone, and as she had so many times in the past, gave thundering voice to the voiceless, both slave and female.

After officially addressing the attendees, Lucretia presented the slate of officers. The women selected represented the diversity and accomplishments of those gathered. There was a president, six vice presidents, and four secretaries. Mary S. Parker, president of the Boston Female Anti-Slavery Society, was elected president of the convention. She had been among the courageous women who faced down an anti-abolitionist mob in Boston in 1835. A contemporary wrote of her, "The same voice which for a moment allayed the fury of a portion of the Boston mob threw sanctity over this consecrated assembly."[19]

The vice presidents were equally impressive. Lucretia Mott and Sarah and Grace Douglass were among them. As was Ann C. Smith, an abolitionist from Peterborough,

New York, who was active with her husband Gerritt Smith in the Underground Railroad and supported justice for Native Americans. Abby Ann Cox, from New York City, was known for her more traditional views—not just about integration but also morality. Confirming women's role in shaping their families' moral life, she joined Rebecca Buffum Spring in putting forth a resolution clarifying the responsibilities of women to help the abolitionist cause by shaping the consciousness of the next generation.

Lydia Maria Child, the last of the vice presidents, was one of the most prolific authors of the day. Her books were wildly popular. She wrote novels, a book of household advice, and a three-volume study of world religions. Child would go on to use the power of her pen for the cause. In her lifetime, she published fifty-eight books.

The four secretaries were Angelina Grimké; Mary Grew, who had set the convention in motion; Maria Weston Chapman's sister, Anne Weston, a member of the Boston Society who organized fundraising events; and Sarah Pugh, who had founded a progressive elementary school in Philadelphia.

The conveners were well aware that they faced strong opposition. Their beliefs and actions were not just a threat to racist American society but to patriarchal political and religious institutions. Perhaps for that reason, the convention began with a reading of the Twenty-Seventh Psalm, calling down transcendent energies from the biblical writings: "The Lord is the stronghold of my life. . . . Tho an army besiege me, my heart will not fear, tho war break out against me, even then will I be confident."

After prayer, Sarah Grimké rose and stated the purpose of the meeting: to organize women throughout the free states and "establish a system of operations" to end slavery. No one objected, and as the invitation was given for each delegate to enroll her name as a member of the convention, they stepped forward one by one, pledging their commitment.

The elected delegates came from antislavery societies in seven states: New Hampshire, Massachusetts, Rhode Island, New York, New Jersey, Pennsylvania, and Ohio. Another 104 women were corresponding members, adding another three states to those represented. Following the enrollment, four letters of good wishes were read, which helped set the tone. The first was from Maria Weston Chapman, who had conceived the idea of the convention, but at the last minute was unable to attend. She wrote:

Beloved Friends,

We doubly owe to the slave this Convention, the first general one of women ever held in our country, if not in the world. . . . [W]e owe it to the world which has so deeply concerned itself with our proceedings on the abolition question, to declare what are the principles and measures which we adopt. We owe it to ourselves to do it with one accord in solemn assembly, by the utterance of deep thoughts and powerful words; and to our Maker to do it with earnest prayer.

I am ever yours for the enslaved,
Maria Weston Chapman

In the second letter, Mary Clark, writing from Concord, New Hampshire, pledged her support:

Respected and Beloved,

. . . So great is the unanimity among New Hampshire female abolitionists, and so much are they in harmony with the great mass, that we are confident they will concur in whatever general measures you may see meet to adopt, and respond to whatever resolutions may be passed in your convention.

Mary Clark

The third letter was written by Maria Sturges from Putnam, Ohio, who corresponded regularly with abolitionists in the Northeast:

Dear Friends,

. . . If woman is ever called upon to arise in all the majesty of virtue, and lift up her voice against any prevailing system of inequity, it is when woman is made the victim of brutal lust and unlimited power [by slavery]. . . . Whether we regard it in the light of patriotism or religion, we are called upon by all that we hold dear in both to employ the gentle, yet omnipotent force of truth for its overthrow.

Yours in behalf of the oppressed,
Maria Sturges

Finally, there was a letter of support from a British women's abolitionist group, demonstrating that the sisterhood reached across the ocean.

> To the Ladies of the American Anti-Slavery Societies,
> Dear Sisters,
>
> . . . When clouds of discouragement arise to darken your horizon, we would remind you of the immutable promises of God's own word: "For the oppression of the poor, now will I arise, sayeth the Lord." . . . Go on then, beloved sisters, in the strength of the Lord, pursue your noble work, till slavery, with the odious and un-Christian distinction of color, be no longer known amongst you.
>
> Maria Smith[20]

With these words resounding in the church, the women got down to business. Over the next three days, they debated and adopted fifty-two resolutions drafted by the ten-member Committee of Arrangements. Most were accepted unanimously.

Child joined with the Grimké sisters to prepare nine of the resolutions presented the first day, many of which established the broad parameters of their abolitionist position.

The first resolution articulated the spiritual foundation of abolition, stating that abolition was "the cause of God, who created mankind free, and of Christ who died to redeem them from every yoke" and that it was the duty of all to "uphold freedom; thus showing the love and gratitude of the Great Redeemer by treading in his steps." At the outset, they affirmed that they were called by God and were doing God's work on earth. It was a rousing way to begin the voting.

The second resolution, presented by Child, articulated the women's fundamental philosophy: the principle of human rights for all. Their issue was not solely the maltreatment of slaves, as many argued that some slaves were treated well, and even boasted about it. Rather, the women insisted that no person should own another and "no compromise can be made on the score of kind usage, while man is held as property of man."[21] The only righteous response to slavery was immediate abolition.

The third, fourth, and fifth resolutions, proposed by Angelina Grimké, denounced Northern collusion with Southern slavery—challenging Congress's denial of the right of the abolitionists to petition, condemning Northerners for marrying slaveholders, and urging the repeal of Northern laws that protected slavery. All passed with unanimous votes.

In the sixth resolution, Sarah Grimké took the matter of collusion a daring step further, condemning Northern women who married slaveholders, in the process "identifying themselves with a system which desecrates the marriage relations among a large portion of the white inhabitants of the Southern states, and utterly destroys it among the victims of their oppression."

The seventh resolution, also presented by Child, challenged state laws that allowed slaveholders traveling in the North to retain ownership of their slaves as they visited. It also called for the passage of laws by legislatures of Northern states guaranteeing fugitive slaves the right to trial by jury.

The atmosphere of unity and resolve was electrifying as the first seven resolutions passed. Like skipping stones along the unbroken mirror of a lake, they had been fighting lonely battles for years, on their own and in small societies, struggling to make even the smallest difference. Now here, together, they were creating an enormous wave.

In the waning hour of the convention's first day, two resolutions presented by Angelina and Sarah Grimké at last put forth the role of women in the most direct manner. Sarah's eighth resolution was innocuous and didn't even reach a vote. But when Angelina stood at the lectern and read the ninth resolution with a clear voice, the hall fell silent as the women grappled with its searing consequence:

> Resolved: That as certain rights and duties are common to all moral beings, the time has come for woman to move in that sphere which Providence has assigned her, and no longer remain satisfied in these circumscribed limits with which corrupt custom and a perverted application of scripture have encircled her; therefore that it is the duty of woman, and the province of woman, to plead the cause of the oppressed in our land, and to do all that she can by her voice, her pen, and her purse, and influence of her example, to overthrow the horrible system of American slavery.[22]

Angelina believed that women could no longer accept the "circumscribed limits" of corrupt custom and a perverted application of scripture when duty compelled them to use all of their resources to fight the scourge of slavery.

And with this resolution, they entered the political arena as their duty and right.

There was a stirring in the body of the convention, an uncomfortable rumble of dissent. This resolution was the third rail for some women. For while they believed fiercely in the cause of abolition, they either dismissed the connection to women's equality or felt it was too treacherous to follow that path. It was, as Lucretia Mott would later tell her friend and colleague Elizabeth Cady Stanton, the first public call for women's rights in America. And as such it did not sit well with the traditionalists in the room.

Unlike other resolutions, which were enthusiastically endorsed, this one hit a nerve. Debate was intense. For some of the women, the idea of broadening women's roles beyond the home and family violated their sense of propriety. The difference of opinion over the resolution on women's rights created palpable tension at the convention. Though unified in their stance against slavery, they remained divided over the question of women's larger role in society. Women had long served under the guise of benevolent societies, church groups, and other volunteer organizations. With Angelina's resolution, a new declaration was made. In essence, she was asking the women to see their rights as citizens as fully equal to those of their husbands, fathers, and brothers, their voices just as important in shaping political decisions and national laws. While this excited many women, it made others uneasy and even angry.

The dissenting women spoke for many, including the majority of religious leaders, who feared that disrupting the social balance created by the sexual division of labor would actually destroy civilization. The theory of separate spheres—that men's world was public and women's domestic—was largely unquestioned. This separation by gender kept women isolated from public power, but simultaneously reflected respect for female emotion and intuition by according women authority in the areas of religion, morality, and child rearing. For Angelina and others, it provided a bridge over which a small percentage of women would cross to take on reform issues such as abolition. Having moral responsibility within the family gave them a foothold in their climb toward more authority in society.

Herein was the impasse. The cult of true womanhood, which had emerged out of the separate spheres concept, suggested that a woman's fullest development occurred when she focused on her significant influence at home. There were two schools of thought on the matter. While some interpreted the cult of true womanhood as an ideology that kept women barred from public life, others thought of it as a progression in both women's psychological development and their greater social empowerment. It is easy to understand how some women could fight for the abolition of slavery and yet object to this resolution advocating women's public responsibilities.

Although the very act of forming a separate female society (and rejecting the idea promulgated in male societies that women could not be fully heard in this matter) made the question of women's status relevant, some of the women gathered still resisted a call to equality. They did not grasp the dissonance of advocating for freedom of one class of society while being denied themselves. Nor did they appreciate that the convention itself gave lie to the idea that women's proper place was in the home, not in the public sphere. For there they were!

By putting forth her resolution, Angelina was attempting to place advocacy for women on the same plane as advocacy for the slave. It was a bridge too far for many women, who could accept a moral mandate to help those enslaved by a sinful society, but could not yet see that the sin touched their lives as well. So engrossed were they in the present that they couldn't imagine a time in the future when, their cause fulfilled, they would be returned to their hearths, their own plight unchanged. But that was exactly the future Angelina was capable of imagining—and was trying to change.

When the resolution was called for a vote, twelve women voted no. It passed, but was the only one that did not receive unanimous support. The convention adjourned for the day with a small tear in the fabric of its unity.

As the second day of the convention dawned, the twelve members who had dissented from Angelina's resolution moved that it be reconsidered. The motion was denied, but the issue was not abandoned. The women all recognized that there needed to be a bridge between the two positions.

Abby Ann Cox and Rebecca Buffum Spring, two of the dissenters, found a way. In the afternoon, they rose to present a resolution promoting a new mandate for women, which respected their traditional role while giving them a critical way to make a difference. The mandate called on women to raise their children to be abolitionists, and it passed with great enthusiasm. Thus both views were incorporated, and the rift was mended. In this way the women demonstrated their ability to reach across disparate views and experiences to achieve a loving and supportive compromise, if not a consensus.

Although politically inexperienced, the convention attendees were intuitively wise. They understood that the meaning of their sisterhood was not to close doors but to reach out with openness toward those with differing views. The convention was not about sameness or creating a singular party line but rather about creating space where different perspectives could coexist—a place for all abolitionist sisters. Differences emerged. Tempers flared. Tension existed between the women of color and some white women. But the commitment to freedom allowed the women to create a caring space. The controversy over the public or private nature of women's roles became a harbinger of the larger public debate that would emerge in the coming years. But for now the women sought and found common ground on the great moral issue of the day and focused their attentions on the practical matters of what they would and *could* do. Their capacity for unity, even in the face of dissent, was the nurturing centerpiece of their activism—the foundational principle of their blueprint. In opening their hearts to one another, they made their holy mission possible.

CHAPTER THREE
A PUBLIC VOICE

The cure for all the ills and wrongs, the cares,
the sorrows, and the crimes of humanity, all lie
in the one word "love." It is the divine vitality that
everywhere produces and restores life.

—LYDIA MARIA CHILD

The hearts and minds of the attendees of the 1837 convention were never far from their British sisters who, in pioneering the idea of antislavery petitions, had literally brought their nation to heel. They were bold and made their presence known, adopting an original Wedgwood cameo image featuring a kneeling female slave as their logo. It was captioned, "Am I Not a Woman and a Sister."

But it was the British women's petition drives, not their medallions, that unleashed their power. In 1833 petitions bearing the signatures of nearly three hundred thousand women had been delivered to the British Parliament, allegedly provoking one member to say, "We can delay no longer. When all the maids and matrons of England are knocking at our doors, it is time for us to legislate."[1] Soon after, the Parliament passed the Abolition of Slavery Act. This was a model the women of America were eager to emulate.

At the 1837 convention, Lydia Maria Child spearheaded the effort to launch a national petition drive with her *Circular to the Female Anti-Slavery Societies in the United States*. She had become one of the brightest lights of the convention—a woman of achievement with a ringing voice and a deft pen. As the youngest of six children growing up in Medford, Massachusetts, outside of Boston, she longed to be educated like her beloved brother Convers, who was eight years older. Since the doors of institutional learning were not open to her, Convers tutored her in literature, philosophy, history, religion, and science. He would later introduce her to thinkers such as the transcendentalist Ralph Waldo Emerson, whom Convers hosted in his home.

As a young woman, she asked to be baptized Maria instead of her given name, Lydia. This was an early example of the independence that characterized her life. Such autonomy was hard to express in an environment where her life was not her own. Maria's greatest dream was to follow her brother to school when he left for Harvard. Instead, she was sent to Maine to live with her married sister. Outrage over this inequity, combined with her experiences observing the native peoples in Maine, galvanized Maria on issues of equality. In the condemnation of the

Cherokees by seemingly virtuous Puritans, she saw only a horrifying bigotry, far removed from Christian principles. With their "simplicity, hospitality, and generosity," she wrote, the Cherokees were closer than the Puritans to the "pure religion of Jesus."[2] This budding awareness of the sins of racism laid the groundwork for a lifelong pursuit of equality for all those excluded by society.

Her ideas could be quite radical. When she was twenty-two, Maria wrote her first novel, *Hobomok*. The book was controversial because of its subject matter—a passionate relationship between a white woman and a noble Native American warrior. The book's stunning success threw Maria into the cultural and literary spotlight. Over time, she wrote other novels with the same theme of individuals in mixed-race relationships. The stories reflected her belief that integration would be the ultimate solution to racism in the culture.

In the coming years she produced several successful novels and a popular handbook on household management, *The Frugal Housewife*, which was also popular in England and Germany. She started a bimonthly magazine for children, *Juvenile Miscellany*, the first of its kind. During this time, she ran a private school and met her future husband David, an attorney.

Her books became best sellers, and Maria was accepted into the best literary circles. But all of that would change when she took on abolition as her life's calling. In 1831 she and David became inspired by the writings of William Lloyd Garrison to embrace the abolition cause. Two years later, when Maria wrote the abolitionist treatise *An Appeal in Favor of That Class of Americans Called Afri-*

cans, her audience abandoned her. Sales of *The Frugal Housewife* plummeted, *Juvenile Miscellany* ceased publication, and many literary colleagues deserted her. Her income dwindled. The Boston library even canceled her privileges. The consequences of taking a stand against slavery were bitter, yet Maria remained committed—the moral choice was clear. Vowing to "work in my own way, according to the light that is in me," she devoted herself to the cause.

At the 1837 convention, Maria outlined the most ambitious plan for their endeavor. Her *Circular* instructed the societies to disseminate antislavery petitions throughout the towns and villages of the free states. By mounting a national campaign with standardized petitions and procedures, they would send so many petitions that Congress could not ignore them. The *Circular* began,

> Dear Sisters, The Anti-Slavery Convention of American Women have appointed a committee to confer with you concerning the righteous cause, in which all our hearts are deeply interested. . . . We all feel that duty to God, and to our fellow-beings, require us to do something for the suffering slaves. . . . Be not persuaded that your petitions will be useless because they are signed by women.[3]

The *Circular* encouraged the women to talk to everyone they met with the zeal of evangelists. It also mentioned the "Hon. Mr. Peyton, member of Congress from slaveholding Tennessee, who assured one of our friends that he dreaded the influence of women on this subject more than any other influence."

After Maria made this presentation, the attendees were called in rotation to pledge themselves to the effort. This was an important moment. Petition writing by American women was a recent activity. This roll call provided the opportunity for each woman to step forward and announce her commitment to a political tactic that planted her squarely in the public sphere. Given that women had almost no rights of citizenship, including but not limited to the vote, and were culturally denied public speech, here was a powerful way to exercise their voice.

Three central committees were appointed to oversee the spread of the *Circular* and the petitions, as well as to answer questions. The first committee, headed by Maria Weston Chapman, Henrietta Sargent, and Catherine Sullivan, was focused in Boston. There was also a Philadelphia petition campaign, directed by Sarah Douglass, Sarah Pugh, and Mary Grew; and a New York campaign, directed by Rebecca Spring, Juliana Tappan, and Anna Blackwell.

Committees were also formed to prepare documents for wide distribution. These documents are among the earliest political writings by women in America's history. Teams of three women were assigned to create each of six documents:

1. The *Appeal to the Women of the Nominally Free States* was a polemical piece exhorting the nation to wake up to its own hypocritical public policy on race and gender.
2. The *Address to Free Colored Americans* asserted that the issue was not just slavery but also rac-

ism. It was time for the black population to take equal place.

3. The *Letter to the Women of Great Britain* reflected the international nature of their political organizing.

4. The *Circular to the Female Anti-Slavery Societies in the United States* declared, "When all the maids and matrons of the land knock at the door of Congress, our statesmen must legislate." (This was Child's.)

5. The *Letter to the Juvenile Anti-Slavery Societies* reflected their intention to inspire the next generation. (This letter, unfortunately, was lost.)

6. The *Letter to John Quincy Adams* reflects their determination to engage one-on-one with top governmental leaders.

Before the convention's conclusion, several other resolutions were brought forward. One had to do with colonization, the growing idea that all black people, free or enslaved, should be moved to other countries. The women went on record protesting the principles of the American Colonization Society. Condemning colonization as "anti-Republican and anti-Christian," the record states that the resolution "elicited much expression of opinion, and some touching appeals from the colored members of the Convention." At this moment, black and white women together formed an interracial political dialogue that was rare in the nineteenth century. The language of this resolution promised "to *unite* our efforts for the accomplishment of the holy object of our association."[4]

These vows emboldened the women to believe that their country, which seemed hopelessly ideologically split, could be reconciled. Nothing less than the soul of society was at stake.

As the convention came to a close, the women pledged to raise money for the work they were undertaking. They collected $357.50 to print the proceedings and circulate them to all female antislavery groups. Mary Grew then moved that they meet at the same time the following year. In agreement, the women decided to convene in 1838, at the soon-to-open Pennsylvania Hall in Philadelphia, which abolitionists were building to house groups that worked for social justice.

The women also vowed to stay active in their societies and to continue working collaboratively to strengthen their individual efforts. Men were functioning in forums similar to these conventions, but with far less emphasis on collaboration. Yet collaboration, intuitively adopted and modeled by these women, is what the country desperately needed. Divided in a way the young country had never experienced, it needed this new paradigm to mend the breech that widened each day between North and South.

Women's presence in a public, political forum was radical in and of itself. They had instituted a new organizational style based on connection, including interracial membership and leadership. They worked together—in relation to each other—allowing for diversity of race and opinion to exist side by side. Rather than belittling or blocking ideas different from their own, they were able to maintain a respect for one another, and dialogued until they found ideas and language that worked for the vast majority.

In the final resolution of the 1837 convention, Maria called upon the women to "stand pledged to each other and the world, to *unite* our efforts for the accomplishment of the holy object of our association, that herein seeking to be directed by divine wisdom, we may be qualified to wield the sword of the spirit in this warfare; praying that it may never return to its sheath until liberty is proclaimed to the captive."[5]

As the women streamed out of the hall, their minds already traveling home with thoughts of the work ahead of them, they hoped their mission would be a healing force in communities and families that had been sharply divided by the issue of slavery. They were unwavering in their justification for such a holy truce: that slavery was a sin, in conflict with the law of God; that it was in conflict with the constitutional law of equality and freedom; that abolition was a holy duty, both politically and spiritually; and that sympathy for the slave could bring about harmony and social cohesion.

More than just a deeply flawed social and economic system, slavery was a spiritual transgression that "throws confusion into the arrangements of Infinite Wisdom, breaks up the divine harmony, and tears the very foundations of human society. It produces a state of things at war with nature." Slavery violated constitutional and sacred law, and Northerners shared the stain. As the women wrote,

Can crime be fashionable and common in one part of the Union and unrebuked by the other without corrupting the very heart's blood of the nation, and lowering the standard of morality everywhere?

[O]ur country from Maine to Florida is more or less connected with, and involved in, the awful sin of slavery, "the blood of the poor innocents is found on our skirts," the free states are partakers with those who rob God of his creatures, for although most of them have nominally no slaves on their soil, they do deliver unto slaveholders the servant that is escaped from his master, in direct violation of the command of Jehovah.[6]

Thus, they viewed abolition as their "high and holy duty." Theirs was a battle against the sin of all sins. They wrote in the convention paper that this duty was "above all to their God." The designation of abolition work as "holy" sanctified their actions, inspiring them to cultivate their greatest strength and wisdom. Abolition was a sacred mission and a religious vocation:

Our weapons are not carnal, but spiritual: we wield no other sword than the sword of the Spirit; we encounter the foes of freedom with the word of God, whilst our feet are shod with the preparation of the Gospel of peace . . . and we know that Truth is mighty and will prevail.[7]

They felt armed by God. Disillusioned by the many ecclesiastical and legal entities that supported slavery, abolitionist women turned instead to their own intuitive faith. They lived the ideal that a moral person must convert feelings into words, words into actions:

Shall woman stand by and see all this in silence and in inaction—shall she feel all this, and shall she not speak? Shall her soul glow within her like a furnace of fire, and leap into her mouth, and force an utterance for itself by burning its way outward, and must she smother it, must she quench it, because the south threatens that the tongue which utters the truth shall be torn out and thrown upon a dunghill? If she should hold her peace, the stones would immediately cry out![8]

This was a clever reframing of Jesus's own words—that if his followers failed to sing praise to God, the very stones would cry out. And now the women were speaking out—in a full-throated way.

One of their greatest weapons was the idea of sympathy as that aspect of humanity that could heal slavery's divisiveness. "The sympathy we feel for our oppressed fellow citizens who are enslaved in these United States," they declared in their *Address*, "has called us together."

Sympathy was the motivating force. It moved them to attempt to connect to the pain of slavery and it established their connection to one another. And it was this sympathy that compelled them to attend the convention. Once in connection, the women realized that sympathy could be used to increase the ranks of abolitionists. Feeling the injustices of slavery at the soul level, as the slave felt it, would lead to change. And thus it had the power to restore the original harmony of God.

ANGELINA GRIMKÉ'S VERDICT on the success of the meeting was rapturous: "Such a convention as this, the world never saw," she declared. For the first time, women were empowered to think, speak, and act politically. After the convention, Angelina wrote to her friend Jane Smith:

> I think we were greatly favored in getting along as well as we did; much more was said in the way of debate than I expected, & this contributed very much to the animation & interest of the meetings, & very soon broke down all stiffness & reserve, threw open our hearts to each other's view, and produced a degree of confidence in ourselves & each other which was very essential & delightful. Some of our Resolutions will certainly frighten the weak & startle the slumbering, particularly those on Southern intermarriages, the province of woman, and the right of Petition.[9]

The women believed that taking up the sacred work of justice would create a quickly spreading contagion of support for immediate abolition. In the *New Hampshire Herald of Freedom*, another woman described the power of the convention and its potential to elevate women:

> The relics of pro-slavery which found their way to this assembly, were slivered by the sword of truth skillfully wielded by the power of women. There was a depth of intellect—a warmth of feeling—a unity of spirit—and an energy of soul most beautifully combined. . . . The female convention will, I think, do much toward elevating the females of America to that rank . . . they should from the morning of our independence have aspired.

A Boston delegate recognized the historic significance of

the meeting in a report to the Boston Female Anti-Slavery Society, published in June 1837 in the *Liberator*:

> Thus ended the first general convention of women ever held in America: but its influences strike far into the future. Long after slavery shall have become a word to be found only in old books; long after the practice of separate meetings of men and women for the discussion of great principles shall have disappeared, it will be recognized as among the first of the grand series of movements which are to make this enslaved earth again a paradise.

In the larger society, however, this great excitement was dismissed and the high purpose brought back to earth by hostile and derogatory critiques. While history's lens shows the women as visionary and forward-thinking, in their own time they were greeted by a fierce backlash. Scathing articles appeared in the popular press. In the same June 1837 issue of the *Liberator,* one reporter called the meeting "an Amazonian farce," attended by "a monstrous regimen of women":

> The convention to which we refer, was nothing less than A GRAND FEMALE ABOLITION CONVENTION. Yes, most unbelieving reader; it is a fact of most ludicrous solemnity, that our female brethren from all quarters of this most exceedingly happy Union, have been lifting up their voices. . . . The spinster has thrown aside her distaff—the blooming beauty her guitar—the matron her darning needle—the sweet novelist her crow-quill; The young mother has left her baby to nestle alone in

the cradle—and the kitchen maid her pots and frying pans—to discuss the weighty matters of state.

An article in the *New York Herald,* on May 10, ridiculed them:

> It is a magnificent sight to see a large church filled with beautiful women. It is a beautiful sight to see their eyes sparkling with enthusiasm and their rosy cheeks mantling with the warm glow of charity. Though the object be black or white, Otaheitan or Hottentot, right or wrong, feasible or chimerical, women's philosophy is beautiful. But abolition is NO GO. . . . The flaming reports, the hackneyed speeches, the doleful stories of the abolition leaders, sink powerless to the ground.

These critics mocked, discredited, and humiliated any woman who dared participate. One reporter in the *Boston Morning Post* asked sarcastically, "Why are all the old hens abolitionist? Because not being able to obtain husbands they think they may stand some chance for a negro, if they can only make amalgamation fashionable."[10] (This quote built on the fear many people had of interracial marriage and socializing [called "amalgamation" at the time]. Phrases such as "intimate union," "social equality," and "social intercourse" came to refer to amalgamation. The term "miscegenation" was coined in the Civil War years; Democrats used it to increase fear about Lincoln's Emancipation Proclamation during the election of 1864.)

Abolitionists faced riots, mob action, and slander. With characteristic courage, Angelina Grimké responded, "If persecution is the means which God has ordained for . . . emancipation, then . . . let it come."[11] Yet tensions were mounting, and it was unknown how the public would respond to the specter of women filling their neighborhoods with petitions that might break the evil grip of slavery for good.

IN THE MONTHS following the convention, the petitioners adopted the zeal of tent revivalists in spreading the message to every person possible. When women petitioned, they went door-to-door to solicit signatures from neighbors. They contacted old schoolmates and drank tea with new friends, knowing that these relationships would foster change. It was, in every way, an educational effort. As it was written in the *Circular* of the threefold purpose of converting people to abolitionism, "You not only gain the person's name, but you excite inquiry in her mind and she will excite it in others; thus the little circle imperceptibly widens, until it may embrace a whole town."[12] Ohio Presbyterian Maria Sturges eloquently wrote, "Let every petition . . . be baptized with prayer, and commended with weeping and supplication to Him in whose hands are the hearts of all men, that He would turn the channel of their sympathies from the oppressor to the oppressed."[13] Petitioning also brought women into closer relationship with each other as they met one-on-one in their homes. In the very act of relating with others in such an intimate and domestic setting, they showed that the personal is indeed political.

But, as has been the case throughout history—because of their lesser status—women's contributions in these antislavery campaigns have been lost. Most historians

credited men with the success of the antislavery petition campaign, overlooking women's profound leadership. Historian Susan Marie Zaeske of the University of
Wisconsin corrects this omission in her PhD research,
writing, "Not only did women precede men in organizing
their petitioning, but it is likely that the AAS [American
Anti-Slavery Society] derived its national campaign strategy from the method instituted by the women." In 1837
the male-run American Anti-Slavery Society ordered its
executive committee to organize a national petition campaign. This occurred *after* the women shared their plans
with them.

Petitioning was one of the most effective ways for abolitionist women to enter politics and awaken the nation's
sympathy as they went door-to-door. As the Grimké sisters noted, "The right of petition is the only political right
that women have. . . . The fact that women are denied
the right of voting for members of Congress is but a poor
reason they should also be deprived of the right to petition. . . . If not [given the right to petition], they are mere
slaves." Appealing to the sympathy of the public to per-
suade them to sign, Angelina wrote,

> [L]et the Christian women . . . arise. . . . Let them em-
> body themselves in societies, and send petitions up to
> their different legislatures, entreating their husbands,
> fathers, brothers, and sons to abolish the institution of
> slavery; no longer to subject woman to the scourge and
> the chain, to mental darkness and moral degradation;
> no longer to tear husbands from their wives, and chil-
> dren from their parents; no longer to make men, wom-
> en, and children work without wages; no longer to make

their lives bitter in hard bondage; no longer to reduce American citizens to the abject condition of slaves, of "chattels personal"; no longer to barter the image of God in human shambles.[14]

Petitioning gave women public voice. It empowered them in new ways. An article in the *Liberator* told the story of a man who received a petition form in the mail but did not understand what to do with it. His wife tried to explain it to him, but he was still skeptical. She insisted it could be done. So the man hitched up the horse and they went to town. He was amazed when his wife, going door-to-door, secured 106 signatures.

Petitioners, successful as they were, frequently encountered two types of hostility—anger at the thought of slaves being freed and outrage at women being politically active. Many people feared that freed slaves would compete for jobs and that it was better to keep them in non-paying work. Sarah Grimké wrote of her dispiriting experience petitioning in Fort Lee, New Jersey, "One woman told me she had rather see the slaves all shot than liberated, another said she would sooner sign a petition to have them all hung, than set free; she complained bitterly that she was not paid enough for her work, but thought it all right that black people should work for nothing."[15]

Still, the petitioning efforts advanced, always accompanied by a chorus of ridicule. Small groups would gather, shouting, "Go home and spin!" Some townsfolk made crude comments, insinuating that petitioners were sexually promiscuous or perverse. Vulgar accusations were made that the "spinster" petitioners were after "nigger husbands." But they also met many who were willing to sign. This was the first time women had had the opportunity to express their political opinions and thousands were drawn to do so.

Despite this tension, and perhaps even spurred on by it, the women plunged headlong into the national petition campaign, bruised but never dissuaded by the challenge. Lucy Chase, a teacher from Massachusetts, reported that circulating petitions was "disagreeable because so few are willing to sign." The young New Yorker Juliana Tappan, disseminating petitions in her town, was surprised at the ignorance of women on political issues: "Ladies sitting on splendid sofas looked at us as if they had never heard the word Texas and I presume some of them would be unable to say whether it was north or west or south of Louisiana, or whether or not it belonged to the United States." Lydia Buffum, a Quaker from New Jersey, wrote in her diary,

> We women and girls determined that every woman in the place should have a chance to petition congress to abolish slavery. . . . [W]hat a sight of ignorance we found, many thinking there were not slaves in the country. We found it easier to get those who had intelligence to sign our petition. We were never mobbed but sometimes we had threats.[16]

The women persevered, however, and before long Congress was flooded with petitions. There were so many that they were piled on the tables, under the tables, and in storage bins. Some were allegedly used as fuel for fire. One observer commented, "[T]he time of several clerks is wholly occupied with them alone. They are stowed away in the antechambers by wagon loads, and ere long there will be almost a sufficient quantity to erect a pyramid that shall vie with the proudest on the plains of Egypt as a great moral monument to the expressed will of a free people." The poet John Greenleaf Whittier wrote to his sister, "By the time Congress meets, there will be petitions enough to break all the tables in the Capitol, ready for delivery." Over half the petitions that poured in were signed by women. Senator Robert James Walker of Tennessee said that he was "pained to see the names of so many American females" on petitions, as reported in the Congressional record:

> It appeared to him exceedingly indelicate that sensitive females of shrinking modesty should present their names here as petitioners, in relation to the domestic institutions of the South, or of the District. Surely they would be much better employed in attending to their domestic duties as mothers, sisters, wives, and daughters, than in interfering with a matter in regard to which they were entirely ignorant. Mr. W. said, he believes it the ladies . . . would let us alone, there would be but few abolition petitions.[7]

Virginia Congressman James Bouldin also resisted the onslaught, insisting that petitions should be ignored. His condescending words on January 12, 1836, recorded in the *Congressional Globe*, reflected a great deal about the prevailing views of women as participants in the political process:

Look to the sources of their information. They rely in a great measure on the representations of the ladies, who appear to be the principal petitioners. Let me cast no slur over any portion of the fair sex. I wish them every good wish if they be single, which I must believe is generally their condition; if they had husbands and children, they would find something else to do—I wish them all good husbands and something better to do.

In 1836 Congressman Henry Laurens Pinckney from South Carolina introduced legislation to table the anti-slavery petitions. His legislation became known as the "Pinckney Gag Law." It was followed by a yearly gag resolution until the refusal to accept antislavery petitions became a standing rule of the House in 1840.

Refusing to back down, abolitionists insisted that this congressional act infringed upon their human rights. On this point, the antislavery women had an ally. "Old Man Eloquent," as Congressman John Quincy Adams was called, opposed the gag rule. But when they sent a letter thanking him for defending their right to petition, they also challenged him to support the abolition of slavery in the District of Columbia. So strong were they in their convictions, they dared confront the man who had been president of the United States. And they did not let up on their petition drive.

The number of women's signatures on petitions grew steadily, from fifteen thousand signatures in 1836 to well over two hundred thousand signatures after the 1837 convention. In 1838 petitions to Congress were stacked to the ceiling in a room twenty feet by thirty feet by fourteen feet. The petitions kept coming, even after Congress refused to accept them, but they were no longer counted or recorded. The petitions simply disappeared.

WITH THEIR WRITING and their role as officers at the convention, Sarah and Angelina Grimké were gaining full voice. Soon after the convention, they set out on what would become one of the most extraordinary public speaking tours of the century. In the course of their New England tour, which ran late May through December 1837, the sisters addressed almost ninety audiences in sixty-seven towns—more than 40,500 people.

They attracted large crowds of women and men. Audiences were diverse, from the working class to top politicians. The turnout for their debut in Dorchester, Massachusetts, was so large that organizers moved the meeting site from a private residence to the town hall. At Roxbury, Massachusetts, the Grimkés spoke to nearly three hundred women and men; at Lowell, Massachusetts, over fifteen hundred. Their three lectures in Salem drew twenty-four hundred. In a mill town like Lowell, the spirit of independence was taking hold in the new working class. Women working in the mills were organizing for increased pay and lining up to sign antislavery petitions. Angelina recounts her experience lecturing to this group:

> Sister says that before I rose I looked as if I was saying to myself "the time has come and the sacrifice must be offered." Indeed I often feel in our meetings as if I was "as a lamb led to the slaughter," sometimes so sick before I rise that it seems impossible for me to speak 10 minutes;

but the Lord is at my right hand, I lean on the arm of [God] and he sustains me and fills my mouth as soon as I open it in faith for the dumb.[18]

By all accounts, the sisters were brilliant together, amplifying each other's strengths. They worked intuitively as a unit, alternating with one another in pioneering uncharted territory for women. Their message to their audiences was not just about abolition; it was also about the power of sisterhood.

As the first women to speak out publicly as reformers, they faced harsh criticism. The worst was from those who thought public speaking was defeminizing and that women reformers had somehow unsexed themselves. A prominent pastor said he would "sooner rob a hen-roost than hear a woman speaking in public."[19] Opinion against them became so hostile that, in a letter to a friend, Lydia Maria Child noted that Angelina was referred to by many as "Devil-ina."

ONE OF THE people who was taking special notice of Angelina's gifts was an activist named Theodore Weld, whom Angelina had met in 1836. A fiery spokesman for the American Anti-Slavery Society, Theodore had made a name for himself for his fearlessness and his ability to calm the frequent mobs that erupted on the lecture circuit. Angelina admiringly referred to him as the "lion of the tribe of abolition." Angelina and Theodore began a meaningful correspondence, in which they shared their deepest religious ideals and their shared goal to see equality for all. Angelina was especially heartened by Theodore's unflinching acceptance of the absolute equality of women with men, a rare notion for the times.

Yet in the months following the 1837 convention, as Angelina and Sarah poured out their views in speeches, public debates, letters, and essays, Theodore seemed to be pulling away. Things came to a head in July 1837, after Angelina participated in a public debate about the right of women to take to the stage. After the debate, criticism rained down on her. This was not new for Angelina. She was used to the wrath of clergy and lay people alike. More disturbing was the harsh rebuke from abolitionists, who felt that the more important matter of abolition was being subsumed by Angelina and Sarah's quest for women's equality. Whittier, their good friend and abolitionist brother, wrote to the sisters, asking why it was necessary to actually speak out on the subject of women's rights, when their very presence in the public forum was proof they belonged there.

It was a great blow to Angelina when Theodore adopted the same position. In a letter to the sisters he carefully maneuvered his way around the controversy, first assuring them that he believed wholeheartedly in the equality of women, writing, "woman in EVERY *particular* shares equally with man rights and responsibilities." This declaration, however, served as a pretext to tell the women that they should move away from advocating for women's equality. Speaking out about the rights of free women, he said, distracted from the need to advocate for the rights of enslaved men and women. He called upon them to consecrate your whole bodies, souls and spirits to the greater work which you can do far better and to far better purpose than any body else. . . . Let us all first wake up the nation to lift millions of slaves of both sexes from the dust, and turn them into MEN and then when we all have our hand in, it will be an easy matter to take millions of females from their knees and set them on their feet, or in other words transform them from babies into women.[20]

In effect he was arguing for patience: *your time will come once the slaves are freed.* Like many of his counterparts, Theodore feared that the quest for female equality distracted from the abolitionist cause—and the idea that these human rights can and must be achieved in tandem was little understood. There was little respect for the mutuality of these goals, indeed little understanding of the nature of misogyny, and the promise of "someday, not now" felt empty to Angelina. Rather than embracing both causes in the spirit of equality for *all*, Theodore was urging her to step aside. She was deeply disappointed and even distraught to receive such counseling from the man who had always supported her mission. She felt he and others were completely missing the point. For how could she truly do the work of the movement from the shadows? In a joint letter to Whittier and Weld, she cited the instances when the women were slandered for going about this work—the times they heard that it was a *shame* for women to speak in churches, the times they were told they had no right to speak on the matter of slavery, the times they were told that silence was their province and submission their duty.

If we are to do any good in the Anti Slavery cause, our right to labor in it must be firmly established. . . . [H]ow can we expect to be able to hold meetings much longer when people are so diligently taught to *despise us* for thus stepping out of the "sphere of woman!" Look at this instance: after we had left Groton, the *Abolition* minister there, at a Lyceum meeting, poured out his sarcasm & ridicule upon our heads & among other things said, he would as soon be caught robbing a hen roost as encouraging a woman to lecture. Now, brethren if the leaders of the people thus speak of our labors, *how long will we be allowed to prosecute them?* . . . They utterly deny *our right* to interfere with this or any other moral reform except in the particular way *they* choose to mark out for us to walk in. . . . If we surrender the right to *speak* to the public this year, we must surrender the right to petition next year & the right to *write* the year after and so on. What *then* can *woman* do for the slave when she is herself under the feet of man and shamed into *silence?* . . .

I fully believe that so far from keeping different moral reformations entirely distinct, that no such attempt can ever be successful. . . . [T]hey blend with each other like the colors of the rain bow. . . . As there were prophetesses as well as prophets, so there ought to be now female as well as male ministers.[21]

Angelina's strong words troubled Theodore, who did not want to hurt or demean her. At the same time, he was committed to the notion of appropriateness and continued to argue with Angelina in the months to come, often suggesting that perhaps her zeal was caused by the sin of pride. Only when Angelina was stricken with typhoid fever did he let up, and perhaps her illness lifted the veil from his eyes. For the first time, he acknowledged to himself that he was in love with her. In February 1838 he put his sentiments in a letter, writing, "For a long time, you have had my whole heart." By Victorian standards this was as brash an expression of love as a man could make. He added, "If your heart, Angelina, does not reciprocate my love, I charge you before a risen Lord not to shrink for a moment through fear of giving me pain from declaring to me the whole truth." Angelina did not hesitate. She wrote back somewhat teasingly that Theodore's letter was a great surprise, yet no surprise at all. And she declared that they were, indeed, "two halves of one whole."

But she also said something else. Noting that Theodore's proposal had mentioned her letter to him and Whittier, she wrote,

> You felt then that it was written under tremendous pressure of feelings bursting up with volcanic violence from the bottom of my soul—you felt that it was the first long breath of liberty which my imprisoned spirit dared to respire whilst in pine in hopeless bondage, painting after freedom to think aloud.[22]

It was a critical moment in their relationship. At long last Angelina felt *heard* by Theodore—confident that his proposal was made in the spirit of full respect. However, her joy at her coming marriage was tempered by the implications of her choice. A delighted letter from her mother expressed relief at the marriage:

I shall myself [be] relieved from the same anxiety that has hitherto rested on me. . . . [A]fter you become a Matron, I hope you will feel that retir[e]ment is best suited to your station; and you will desire to retire from the busy scenes of publicity, and to enjoy that happiness which I hope your home will yield you.[23]

Even Angelina's friends in the movement wondered if she would discontinue her work after marriage. Theodore tried to set her mind at ease in one instance. By law, a husband was given control of all of his wife's possessions in a concept called *feme covert*—"woman covered"—or coverture. Coverture was a legal doctrine that made a woman totally dependent on her husband. Upon marriage she lost all rights to income, family inheritance, and property. Children were considered the property of the father, and mothers had no rights to them in cases of separation. This carryover from British common law was in effect unless a husband chose otherwise, and in this case Theodore did, agreeing to sign a prenuptial agreement rejecting a coverture arrangement after marriage and reasserting Angelina's right to control her own material future. He also agreed that they would provide a permanent home for Sarah.

AS WINTER GAVE way to spring, there was an air of anticipation among the female abolitionist societies, who had labored so hard for the cause and for themselves. Their second meeting, this time in Philadelphia, was approaching. After twelve months of petitioning, practicing sympathy, public speaking, agitating for religious reform, and circulating antislavery propaganda, they were ready to gather again, eager to seek counsel, wisdom, and strength from the sisterhood. Angelina and Theodore chose the week of the convention, when those they held most dear would be gathered, to celebrate their wedding.

For Angelina, the political was personal. Thus, it was fitting that she chose to marry Theodore in the setting where her commitment to the abolitionist cause and women's equality was on display. The wedding, which took place in the home of Angelina's recently widowed sister, Anna Frost, was a blending of both abolitionism and feminism.

The guest list included friends and fellow activists both white and black. Six former slaves of the Grimké family attended. Two ministers, one white and one black, were in attendance to bless the couple, and Theodore and Angelina wrote and delivered the vows themselves. As Sarah Grimké later related, "Theodore addressed Angelina in a solemn and tender manner," vowing to renounce all legal authority that laws at the time gave him over Angelina's property, so that their lives would only be ruled by their love, commitment, and the moral authority given by God.[24] Angelina chose to leave the word "obey" out of the vows. They were united, not as leader and follower, or as master and subservient, but as equals.

Because the wedding was not Quaker and Theodore was a Presbyterian, Angelina was expelled from the Quaker meeting for choosing to marry outside the faith, and Sarah was expelled for agreeing to attend the wedding. (Lucretia Mott stayed away for this reason.)

Their mother did not travel from Charleston to attend. What was originally relief that her daughter was marrying must have soon turned to dismay at the egalitarian nature of the union. As the feminist historian Gerda Lerner viewed it, Angelina "was getting married in a manner calculated to shock and dismay the pillars of Charleston society, among whom she had been raised."[25]

In marrying Theodore, Angelina was joining a special society of women whose marriages were built on mutual respect and common beliefs. Such marriages were already being practiced all around her—with Mott and her husband James, Child and her husband David, Maria Weston Chapman and her husband Henry, and Abby Kelley and her husband Stephen. For these women, the intimacy of marriage could not be fully realized without equality. They believed that the very essence of marriage was formed in this partnership. As Lucretia wrote in "Discourse on Women" in 1849, "In the true married relationship, the independence of husband and wife will be equal, their dependence mutual, and their obligations reciprocal." In an era when marriage typically ended a woman's sovereignty, these unions enhanced it.

Not surprisingly, news of the wedding spread throughout Philadelphia, causing an uncharitable reaction. There were rumors that it was an interracial marriage, and although it was not, the mere presence of black guests was viewed as an abomination. While joy surrounded this occasion, the press made a mockery of it, as if to fuel acrimony just before the women's convention began. For example, this newspaper account was reprinted in the June 8, 1838, issue of the *Liberator*:

It is, moreover, currently, and we have reason to believe, accurately rumored that at the wedding of Miss Grimké, one of the itinerant lecturers, who was married in this city . . . the bridal guests consisted of six blacks and six whites, an arrangement which was intended to demonstrate the perfect social equality. These things, aided by the frantic ravings of Garrison, who has been lecturing here, have necessarily led to much excitement, and at the time of writing these paragraphs, we are not without fear that some serious breach of the peace may be the result.

The women and their supporters were well aware of the growing clamor leading up to their convention. Placards had begun to appear around the city, urging citizens to gather and—"forcibly if they must"—prevent the next meeting of the Female Anti-Slavery Society from happening. The dissent was both sexist and racist. The outcry was directed less at the substance of the women's cause than at how boldly they were breaking the most closely held taboos. Not only were they walking the streets, organizing, and speaking openly but they were doing so arm in arm with their black sisters.

On the eve of the second convention, the public sentiment was clear. It would be a fight.

CHAPTER FOUR
FIERY BACKLASH

*Men, brethren and fathers—mothers, daughters
and sisters, what came ye out for to see? A reed
shaken with the wind? . . . There is nothing to be
feared from those who would stop our mouths,
but they themselves should fear and tremble.*

—ANGELINA GRIMKÉ

The day after Angelina's wedding, at ten in the morning, the abolitionist women gathered for their second annual convention at the newly erected Pennsylvania Hall. There they joyfully embraced each other, having bonded across the miles in common effort. Two hundred and three women were named on the rolls, but many others would join them in the coming days, pressing their way into the hall to be a part of this awakening. It was reported by the *Liberator* that as many as six hundred attended the meeting.

Most of the women who had attended the 1837 convention returned, greeting one another with warmth, tears, and cries of amazement at how far their nascent movement had come. They had traveled a journey together, and had much to talk about. But there were new women too—some a product of the "yeast" that had grown from the small beginning, and others part of the thriving Philadelphia antislavery movement. Delegates included Harriet Forten Purvis and her sister Sarah, early members of the Philadelphia Female Anti-Slavery Society who belonged to one of the most influential free black families in Philadelphia. (Harriet's husband Robert was a light-skinned black man, and when he escorted Harriet to Pennsylvania Hall, some people on the street thought they were an interracial couple and expressed outrage.) Susan Paul, a black writer and educator whose students had formed an abolitionist choir that toured throughout Massachusetts, was there. Maria Weston Chapman, who had helped organize the first convention but had been unable to attend, was elated to be present for the second. Mary Parker of Boston was once again elected president, and the roster of officers included two additional women of color: Martha Ball, a member of the Boston Female Anti-Slavery Society; and Hetty Burr, a Philadelphia activist and wife of a local barber who was an outspoken abolitionist.

Laura H. Lovell, a young schoolteacher representing the Fall River, Massachusetts, Female Anti-Slavery Society, came to the convention promising to create a report for her sisters back home. Little did she know that her "Fall River Letter," published in the *Liberator* in June 1838, would become the most gripping and thorough account of the remarkable events that transpired during those days. Laura was a talented recorder, whose detailed, moving, and emotionally honest record was a testament to her thoughtful nature. From the very first moment that she stepped onto the streets of Philadelphia, she observed, "In looking abroad over this beautiful, quiet city, the first impression is that I have found on earth a place where order, harmony, love and freedom prevail; but, a second thought reminds me that I'm nearer than ever to the wretched scenes of slavery, and doubtless many a wave from that broad sea of pollution reaches and washes over even the fair city of Brotherly Love."

Indeed. No city was so emblematic of the vision of freedom and equality as Philadelphia. The women were not so far removed from the beginnings of this nation. They could still imagine the sacrifices offered willingly by those seeking to found a nation on the ideals of "life, liberty, and the pursuit of happiness"—even as those ideals were tarnished by the sin of slavery. Perhaps, they thought, this convention would restore a foundational greatness to the city of brotherly—and sisterly—love.

Fresh from a year of petitioning, the women were primed to elevate their work to new heights. The groundbreaking success of the 1837 convention and the national petition campaign energized everyone's expectations for the upcoming meeting. Having appointed officers and committees, the convention adjourned until the following day.

On Wednesday morning the women returned and began their meeting with a plaintive cry to the heavens, in a reading of the Ninety-Fourth Psalm:

Lord, how long shall the wicked, how long shall the wicked triumph?

How long shall they utter and speak hard things and all the workers of iniquity boast themselves? . . .

They gather themselves together against the soul of the righteous, and condemn the innocent blood.

But the Lord is my defense; and my God is the rock of my refuge.

And he shall bring upon them their own iniquity, and shall cut them off in their own wickedness; yea, the Lord our God shall cut them off.

Even as the women met with the utmost seriousness, the chorus of dissent was building in the city, with inflammatory circulars and crowds of people milling around outside of the hall. One widely distributed circular showed abolitionist women lolling from the windows of the convention hall as prostitutes from a brothel, while on the streets below, interracial couples walked with their children of different colors. This type of public mockery was only a taste of the dissent the women faced. With each passing hour, as Laura reported, a growing group of men began to gather at the building, "prowling about the doors, examining the gas-pipes, and talking in an incendiary manner to groups which they collected around them in the street." Throughout the day, the crowd continued to grow, until many thousands of men and boys surrounded the building.

Inside, however, the positive spirit was so strong, and

the passion for action so great, that it was decided to hold a public meeting on Wednesday night, which would feature speeches by Lucretia Mott, Angelina Grimké, Maria Weston Chapman, Abby Kelley, and William Lloyd Garrison. It was a decision of stunning bravado; by Wednesday it was quite clear that the ever-growing mob was becoming more restless.

Ignoring the raucous dissent outside, the women began the work of making motions. The first came from Juliana Tappan of New York. Juliana, the daughter of the prominent abolitionist leader Lewis Tappan, had distinguished herself in the movement with steely determination and boundless energy. Devoted as she was to abolition, before the convention Juliana had expressed a hope that it be "strictly an Anti-Slavery Convention, and that no attempt will be made to introduce subjects not necessarily connected with our duties to the slave." In other words, women's rights were not to be discussed, even though many slaves were women. As secretary of the convention, she rose to present two forceful motions:

> Resolved: That whatever may be the sacrifice, and whatever other rights may be yielded or denied, we will maintain practically the right of petition, until the slave shall go free, or our energies, like Lovejoy's, are paralyzed in death.[1]

(She was referring to Elijah Lovejoy, an abolitionist writer whose columns against slavery so inflamed the citizens of Illinois that they murdered him and destroyed his press, making him a symbol of the movement.)

Resolved: That for every petition rejected by the National Legislature, during their late session, we will endeavor to send five the present year; and that we will not cease our efforts until the prayers of every woman within the sphere of our influence shall be heard in the halls of Congress on this subject.

The New Englander Mary Spencer, an uncommonly independent woman and religious free thinker, who would go on to become an early entrepreneur, rose to offer a third resolution:

Resolved: That we regard the right of petition as dear and inalienable, and so far from discovering a dictatorial spirit, it is the refuge of the most humble and power less, and true greatness would never turn away from such appeals.

Mary Grew offered perhaps the most sobering resolution of all—for it placed the women in overt opposition to the church. Her resolution called on abolitionists to boycott churches that allowed slaveholders or those involved in the slave trade to be members.

Whereas, the disciples of Christ are commanded to have no fellowship with the "unfruitful works of darkness"; and, whereas, union in His church is the strongest expression of fellowship between men; therefore . . .

Resolved: That it is our duty to keep ourselves separate from those churches which receive to their pulpits and their communion tables, those who buy, sell, or hold as property, the image of the living God.

Mary's resolution was followed by a long debate. Tappan, for one, argued that this was not the time for the women to separate from the churches, and that they could accomplish more for the abolitionist cause by remaining in the churches and working from within. In spite of the debate, Mary's resolution passed by a large majority. Still, the fact that it was not unanimously adopted was a disappointment, and continuing dissent made Mary a lightning rod in a brewing religious schism.

According to the "Fall River Letter," the huge turnout of angry protesters had the Pennsylvania Hall managers unnerved. They appealed to Philadelphia Mayor John Swift for security. He refused to bring in police, citing that, "Ninety-nine out of a hundred of those with whom I converse are against you." Arriving to survey the mob, the mayor stood before them and declared, "I would, fellow citizens, look upon you as my police." It was hardly a comforting thought.

IN HER LETTER, Lovell called Wednesday night's public gathering "a heart thrilling spectacle," as the hall filled to its full capacity of three thousand people. She wrote of the diversity of the assemblage—from the warm energies of youth to the steady presence of the old, from the intelligentsia to the reformed slaveholder—"all filled with one mighty purpose."

As Garrison rose to speak, the angry crowd outside

began an assault on the building. Rocks thudded against the brick and broke through the windows, but no one moved as Garrison continued for a half an hour.

As the cacophony of shouts and breaking glass continued, Maria Chapman stood. She must have been recalling her prior experience with a ferocious mob in Boston. Undoubtedly, she also remembered her words at the time: "If this is the last bulwark of freedom, we may as well die here as anywhere."[2] Maria's voice was nearly drowned out by the noise as men from the mob began to batter the door, seeking entry. Male attendees braced themselves against the door as everyone nervously craned their heads and watched.

By this point the attendees had become quite upset and fearful, but the manager of the hall rushed forward to calm them. "It is very important that we keep ourselves calm," he shouted. "The police officers are at the door, and on the least overt act the boys around the house will be secured, and we shall be protected." The audience relaxed a bit, although some might have wondered why the police, if present, were not preventing the hooligans from breaking windows.

Angelina, the main speaker of the evening—and the one the audience most wanted to hear—stepped forward. She did not disappoint, dismissing the mob outside as being powerless against them: "What is a mob? What would the leveling of this Hall be?" she questioned, her voice rising up, clear and powerful, above the noise.

Any evidence that we are wrong or that slavery is a good and wholesome institution? What if the mob should now burst in upon us, break up our meeting and commit violence upon our persons—would this be anything compared with what the slaves endure? No, no: and we do not remember them "as bound with them," if we shrink in the time of peril, or feel unwilling to sacrifice ourselves, if need be, for their sake.[3]

As the building shook and more bricks and stones smashed against the walls and windows, Angelina's voice grew stronger. She spoke from the depths of her own experience as a child of the South against the evils of slavery.

I have seen it—I have seen it. I know it has horrors that can never be described. I was brought up under its wing. I witnessed for many years its demoralizing influences, and its destructiveness to human happiness. It is admitted by some that the slave is not happy under the worst forms of slavery. But I have never seen a happy slave. I have seen him dance in his chains, it is true. But he was not happy.

The crowd outside continued its monstrous roar. Angelina roared back:

There is nothing to be feared from those who would stop our mouths, but they themselves should fear and tremble. The current is even now setting fast against them. If the arm of the North had not caused the Bastille of slavery to totter to its foundation, you would not hear those cries. A few years ago, and the South felt secure, and with a contemptuous sneer asked, "Who are the abolitionists? The abolitionists are nothing?"—Ay, in one sense they were nothing, and they are nothing still. But in this we rejoice, that "God has chosen things that are not to bring to nought things that are."

Garrison later described the moment when Angelina held the enormous crowd in her hands: "As the tumult from without increased, and the brickbats fell thick and fast, her eloquence kindled, her eyes flashed and her cheeks glowed."[4]

Not one woman left the hall. In spite of being nervous and fearful, they would not back down from what they had started. In his *History of Pennsylvania Hall*, Samuel Webb recorded, "This occasion had brought together many of the noblest minds, and of the best and purest hearts among the women of our country, minds capable of grasping, with prevailing strength, subjects of a magnitude and difficulty, which masculine vigor would deem it an honor to master."[5]

Over the noise, Kelley then rose to make her first public speech. She had no prepared remarks. In the Quaker tradition, she stepped forward when she felt moved, and heard herself say,

I have never before addressed a promiscuous [men and women] assembly; nor is it now the maddening rush of those voices, which is the indication of a moral whirlwind, nor is it the crashing of those windows, which is the indication of a moral earthquake, that calls me before you. . . . [I]t is the still small voice within, which may not be withstood, that bids me open my mouth for the dumb—that bids me plead the cause of God's perishing poor.

The mob continued to throw sticks and rocks against the windows as she told the story of Lazarus the beggar. "Look! See him there," she said, as if addressing the slave. "We have long . . . passed by with averted eyes. Ought not we to raise him up?"[6]

In spite of the aura of danger, the evening ended without harm to the attendees. To protect their more vulnerable members, the group of black and white women left the gathering arm in arm, through a hail of rocks and jeers. The women returned to their lodgings, prepared to continue the following morning.

Laura Lovell arrived back at the hall Thursday morning to find a crowd of protesters still gathered. "It was hoped that the sober hours of night would calm the turbulent spirits of the rabble, and bring them under the exercise of reason," she wrote in the "Fall River Letter." "But the scene which the morning presented us was to my mind a full demonstration that the crisis of rage and violence was yet to come."

As the meeting convened, Lucretia Mott stepped forward and called for calm, reminding the women of the courage and perseverance of the early disciples and, smiling warmly at her sisters, urged them to emulate their example. The women continued the work of the convention. Margaret Dye, a Methodist pastor's wife who had been opposed to Grew's resolution the day before, now presented a resolution that reinforced their right to speak for the cause:

Resolved: That the Anti-Slavery enterprise presents one of the most appropriate fields for the exertion of the influence of woman, and that we pledge ourselves, with divine assistance, never to desert the work, while an American slave groans in bondage.

Others followed, formalizing the imperative that mothers teach their children the principles of abolition and "the nature and sanctity of human life"; calling on God's aid in their holy task; establishing a funding protocol to support the work of the movement; and, once again, singling out the "corrupt" church for its support of slavery—as "the system of American slavery is contrary to the laws of God, and the spirit of true religion, and that the church is deeply implicated in this sin, and that it therefore becomes the imperative duty of all her members to petition their ecclesiastical bodies to enter their decided protests against it, and exclude slaveholders from their pulpits and communion tables."

On one of the resolutions, Esther Moore, an elderly Philadelphia woman, made some remarks. She leaned on a cane and, though her voice wavered, her mind was clear, as was her resolve. When she spoke of her abhorrence of slavery even in the days of her childhood, and expressed her deep interest in the cause of emancipation, the younger women felt their hearts lift. Her historical memory and the depth of her conviction, expressed over a long life, moved them to see that the journey, while long, was also enduring.

A meeting was scheduled by another society at the hall that evening, and many of the women were planning to attend. But late in the afternoon the president of the Pennsylvania Hall Association entered the room and suggested that, given the anger of the mob about mixed-race gatherings, "colored sisters not attend the meeting to be held in the hall this evening." Lucretia emphatically rejected this advice. Then an African American conference attendee from New York suddenly rose and insisted, "It would be both selfish and cowardly for my people to shrink in the hour of danger." As recorded in the "Fall River Letter," she went on, "Our friends have suffered much for us and shall we fear to suffer a little for ourselves?" The women applauded her bravery, especially as it was unequivocally true that black women had suffered in ways that white people could not imagine. She was known to have purchased, by her own labor, eleven slaves to deliver them to freedom. She was not going to back down now.

As the meeting came to a close around 4:00 p m , worried male supporters urged the women to leave by a back door so they might escape confrontation with the mob. The women refused. Instead, as abolitionist Bartholomew Fussell recalled in a letter to his nephew Edwin, several chose to make a particularly bold exit:

> At this crisis, a magnanimous act was performed which was more than *manly*, it was indeed *womanly*. Five females came voluntarily out of the convention to speak to the mob, passed through the guard, and went into the midst of the crowd in the street, then separating themselves from each other, they took different positions and stood firm to their purpose like so many monuments of

Virtue, in the midst of corruption, pleading with them for the right to hold their meeting peaceably and for the liberty of the Slave. . . . True, I have never seen the face of an angel, but when they returned to the house their appearance was somewhat superhuman. I shall call it angelic.[7]

Inside the hall, Angelina proposed that they do what they could to offer protection to their black sisters as they walked into the crowd. She suggested the white women take each black woman firmly by the arm. In this fashion they walked out the front door of Pennsylvania Hall, straight into the mob.

Laura described the scene to her Fall River sisters:

We passed out through a mob of two or three thousand, fierce vile looking men and large boys. They allowed us just room to walk, two abreast. We heard the worst language and saw the most hideous countenances, but I believe none were seriously molested. . . . It appeared very rational to conclude, and very evident too from appearances, that the mob was now ripe for some violent outrage. Many threats had been heard from them in the streets, and a great number of them had been exciting their passions for 24 hours by drinking and carousing around the house, and there was no reason to suppose they would do anything less this evening than set fire to the hall. It seemed to me folly and madness to trust ourselves in the power of such evil spirits. They were not to be reasoned with, or treated like rational beings. We should not think it heroic to yield ourselves to the fury of wild beasts.

Meanwhile, the managers of Pennsylvania Hall sent a committee to Mayor Swift, once again pleading with him to provide protection for the building. He told them he would go personally and disperse the crowd himself, as long as they would agree to cancel the evening's meetings, lock the doors, and give him the keys. They agreed. Arriving at the hall, the mayor told the crowd to go home, and then he left. The crowd, however, remained.

As the women enjoyed one another's company in private settings, they were relieved to learn that the mayor had taken the keys and closed Pennsylvania Hall for the night. But shortly before 9:00 p.m., shouts of "Fire!" could be heard on the street. The mob had broken down the doors and set the building ablaze. Many women returned to the street to watch the spectacle. The red-orange glow moved across the faces of the women as they watched (as Laura would record in her "Fall River Letter") the "beautiful building which the diligent acts and hammer had been, for months, patiently rearing; that building which the friends not only of abolition but the friends of free discussion, the friends of civil and religious liberty, the true philanthropist and patriots of our land had reared" go up in flames.

Laura lamented:

What evidence have we in the flames now rising to burnish the heavens above, and spread consternation and terror through this fair city—what melancholy evidence of the wretched state of public morals! How have vice and oppression, villainy and outrage taken the rule! How are the pure and the good driven from the still lovely spot, whose foundations of beauty and order, were laid in peace, and liberty, and love! And where are the magistrates of Philadelphia? Where are the laws which should protect the children of Penn? All, all leagued with this vile mob?

As if in confirmation of Laura's claim, firemen on the scene were observed directing their hoses away from the hall and toward nearby buildings. When the hall finally collapsed, the crowd sent up a booming cry of victory.

ON FRIDAY MORNING, more than one hundred women arrived at a neighboring building, Temperance Hall, to continue their convention. They found the doors locked and the owners denying them entrance for fear that this building would suffer the fate of Pennsylvania Hall. So the women set off, amid jeers from those on the street, taking the long walk to the schoolhouse of their member Sarah Pugh. Once settled there, they felt no danger, but were devastated. Still shaken from the terror of the night before, they formed a circle and began to cite scripture and pray, starting with 2 Corinthians:

> For God, who commanded the light to shine out of darkness, hath shined in our hearts, to give the light of the knowledge of the glory of God in the face of Jesus Christ. But we have this treasure in earthen vessels, that the excellency of the power may be of God, and not of us. We are troubled on every side, yet not distressed; we are perplexed, but not in despair; persecuted, but not forsaken; cast down, but not destroyed.

"We felt," wrote Laura, "a hallowed influence around us." As noted in the *Liberator*'s "Fall River Letter," Mott spoke from the heart about the fear of the previous evening. Hearing that the mob was headed toward her house, and thinking she might be killed, she experienced a moment of truth. "I had often thought how I should sustain myself if called to pass such an ordeal," she told them. "I hope I speak it not in the spirit of boasting when I tell you, my sisters, I believe I was strengthened by God. I felt at the moment that I was willing to suffer whatever the cause required. My best feelings acquit me of shrinking back at the hour of danger. But the mob was not suffered to molest us, and I feel thankful that we slept a few hours in tranquility and peace."

Then they got down to work—determined, even then, even after their convention hall had been reduced to ashes, to finish what they had come to do. Angelina offered an eloquent motion that put the events in perspective:

> Resolved: That we have heard, with grief and shame, of the burning of Pennsylvania Hall, last evening, but rejoice in fullness of hope that God will overrule evil for good, by causing the flames which consumed that beautiful Hall, dedicated to virtue, liberty, and independence, to light up the fires of freedom on every hilltop and in every valley in the state of Pennsylvania, and our country at large.

Not far away, a large crowd was gathering to survey the smoldering ruins of Pennsylvania Hall. As an observer, H. C. W., recounted in the *Liberator*, "Thousands were there exulting in the destruction of the Hall and openly boasting of the share they had in the work." Noting that the women, gathered elsewhere, had continued their work, he praised their courage. "The women have done nobly today. They have held their convention to finish their business, in the midst of the fearful agitating. Their moral daring and heroism are beyond all praise. They are worthy to plead the cause of peace and universal liberty."

In these words, we hear the women's commitment to justice, even in the face of violence. The press and civil authorities had a different opinion of the matter—eager to place the blame on the women themselves, especially for consorting interracially.

The *New York Gazette* editorialized, "The white-skinned damsels who promenaded the streets of Philadelphia arm in arm with their lamp-black paramours . . . are the real authors of this mischief," adding that those "females who so far forget the province of their sex as to perambulate the country" in order to attend national antislavery meetings should be "sent to insane asylums."

In 1838 the *Baltimore Patriot* had a stinging rebuke for the women: "[T]hese fanatics, who are principally female, seem perfectly reckless of the consequences of their acts, however momentous they may be. This nation, we believe, is the only one which presents the disgraceful spectacle of a set of women leaving the sphere of domestic duty to which they belong, and voluntarily agitating . . . arousing the worst passions of the community."

But others saw their heroism. Referring to Angelina's speech at the convention, another account in the *Liberator* stated, "The calmness and impassioned earnestness of Angelina Grimké Weld, speaking nearly an hour 'mid that howling mob, was not surpassed in courage and consecration even by Paul among the wild beasts at Ephesus."

Samuel Webb wrote, "[T]hese American Women passed through the whole without manifesting any sign of fear, as if conscious of their own greatness and of the protecting care of the God of the oppressed."

The Public Ledger, a mainstream Philadelphia periodical with no abolitionist allegiances, nonetheless declaimed the mob attack on Pennsylvania Hall as a "Scandalous Outrage against Law and Decency." The May 18, 1838, issue editorialized, "We are decidedly opposed to any mingling of the two races . . . [but] we should prefer as companions, moral, peaceful and orderly blacks, to profligate and disorderly whites."

The civil authorities did little to find and prosecute the arsonists. The official report, after a long delay, excused the violence because it had been provoked by agitators (the women) advocating for integration. "How else could Philadelphia residents respond," the report concluded, "when confronted by practices 'subversive of the established orders of society,' such as 'the unusual union of black and white walking arm and arm in social intercourse.'"

The incident went to a grand jury, which also exonerated the rioters. The city council concluded that the destruction "was occasioned by the determination of the owners of the building . . . to persevere in openly promulgating and advocating doctrines repulsive to the moral sense of a large majority of our community."[8]

ALTHOUGH PENNSYLVANIA HALL was reduced to rubble, the flames did not leave the movement in ashes. Instead, like sparks leaping from branch to branch in a forest, they spread. But a certain new contentiousness grew out of the events, which would have repercussions for the female antislavery societies.

For those who had spoken against the propriety of women holding conventions, the burning of Pennsylvania Hall must have seemed like confirmation—as if to say, *Look at the trouble you create when you presume to gather in such numbers and from such distances.* In the closing of the "Fall River Letter," Laura addressed this sentiment:

> It has been a question with many, perhaps with some of this Society, whether it is proper for women to hold Conventions. It has been asserted that women are not capable of conducting the business of so large a body as would meet in a Convention. If I may be allowed to judge—not from my own knowledge or sense of propriety, but by a comparison with Conventions conducted by men—I should think all fears of this kind might be dismissed. . . . There was a period when all Ladies' Societies were unknown, but the time came which called for such associated effort—the experiment was tried, and has proved a means of doing much good. In what other way could our Societies prove so efficient, as by meeting annually in Convention? It is worth every thing for Abolitionists, who have such a mighty work to accomplish, to be all acquainted with each other; to be encouraged by each other's zeal and strengthened by each other's strength. . . .

Here, my sisters, is the grand secret of usefulness in the cause. We must feel with the slave and then we must act for him. We must feel ourselves pressed beneath the burden, which bows him to the earth, and then the struggle which we make to cast it off will not be weak and ineffectual; but persevering, strong and energetic.

In her call for perseverance, Laura was acknowledging just how traumatic the events of those convention days were. It was a moment of truth for the young movement. Even as they made inroads in public support—through petitioning, fairs, speaking, and writing—the dissent was growing more overt and violent. They felt in their hearts the darkness before the dawn. They saw their enemies gloating over their seeming victory. And yes, the mob had succeeded in driving the women from Pennsylvania Hall. Not, however, from their cause. They vowed to return to Philadelphia for a third convention in one year's time.

Womens Speaking

Juſtified, Proved and Allowed of by the SCRIPTURES,

All ſuch as ſpeak by the Spirit and Power
of the Lord JESUS.

And how WOMEN were the firſt
that preached the Tidings of the Reſurrection of
JESUS, and were ſent by CHRIST'S
Own Command, before He aſcended
to the Father, *John* 20.17.

---

*And it ſhall come to paß, in the laſt dayes, ſaith the Lord, I will pour out
of my Spirit upon all Fleſh; your Sons and Daughters ſhall Propheſie.*
Acts 2. 27. Joel 2. 28.

It is written in the Prophets, They ſhall be all taught of God, ſaith Chriſt,
John 6. 45.

*And all thy Children ſhall be taught of the Lord, and great ſhall be the
Peace of thy Children.* Iſa. 54. 13.

*And they ſhall teach no more every man his Neighbour, and every man his
Brother, ſaying, Know the Lord ; for they ſhall all know me, from the
leaſt to the greateſt of them, ſaith the Lord.* Jer. 31. 34.

London, Printed in the Year, 1666.

1. As this 1666 edition of Margaret Fell's *Womens
Speaking Justified* shows, women were advocating
for their right and ability to preach, long before the
abolitionist women made the case.

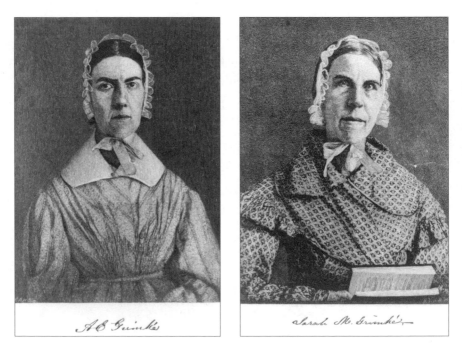

2. Angelina and Sarah Grimké were among the first women to speak and write openly about the evils of slavery. Having been raised in North Carolina in a family of slave owners, they knew too well the suffering and dehumanization the slaves experienced in their daily lives.

3. When the all-male American Anti-Slavery Society refused to allow women a full voice, Lucretia Mott gathered a group of her sisters in a Philadelphia schoolroom and called upon them to create their own female society.

4. In an act of courage, Lucretia Mott arrived at a courthouse and sat next to a black man being charged as a fugitive slave.

5. Sarah Mapps Douglass was
an educator, writer, and abolitionist
who was instrumental in the Female
Anti-Slavery Society. Unlike its male
counterpart, the women's organization
was interracial.

6. One of the founders of the Boston Female Anti-Slavery Society, Maria Weston Chapman had the idea to hold a women's convention, leading to the groundbreaking convention in New York City in May 1837.

Mary Grew

7. As the corresponding secretary of the Philadelphia Female Anti-Slavery Society, Mary Grew began collaborating with Maria Weston Chapman to spread the word of the 1837 women's convention.

Abby Kelley Foster

8. Abby Kelley, from Lynn, Massachusetts, found her voice at the 1838 women's convention in Philadelphia, as a mob outside violently protested the women's gathering—saying, "It is the still, small voice within, which may not be withstood, that bids me open my mouth . . ."

9. Lydia Maria Child was a beloved mainstream author, but when she took on the cause of abolition her career suffered.

10. William Lloyd Garrison's the *Liberator* was a powerful vehicle for advancing the cause of abolition

11. Unable to live with the hypocrisy of a country that upheld freedom for all yet granted it only to white men, the early abolitionist feminists fought tirelessly for their enslaved brothers and sisters.

> **Preamble to the Constitution of the Boston Female Anti-Slavery Society.**
>
> Believing slavery to be a direct violation of the laws of God, and productive of a vast amount of misery and crime; and convinced that its abolition can only be effected by an acknowledgement of the justice and necessity of *immediate emancipation,*—we hereby agree to form ourselves into a Society **TO AID AND ASSIST IN THIS RIGHTEOUS CAUSE AS FAR AS LIES WITHIN OUR POWER.**

12. The Boston Female Anti-Slavery Society was one of the first to be organized, in spite of loud and often violent protests in the community.

> ### EAST INDIA SUGAR.
>
> ———◆———
>
> By six families using East India instead of West India Sugar one Slave less is required: surely to release a fellow-creature from a state of cruel bondage and misery, by so small a sacrifice, is worthy the attention of all.
>
> N.B. The labour of one Slave produces about Ten Cwt. of Sugar annually.
>
> ———◆———
>
> *J. Blackwell, Printer, Iris Office, Sheffield.*

13. Abolitionist women embraced the concept of using their purchasing power to strike an economic blow to slavery.

14. Abolitionist women asked people to have "sympathy" for the slave—to consider how they would feel if their families were torn apart. Here a slave father is sold away from his family.

REBECCA, AUGUSTA and ROSA.
Slave Children from New Orleans

15. For these enslaved children from New Orleans, life was not playful, loving, or free.

16. The Female Anti-Slavery Society held its second convention at Pennsylvania Hall. The women were driven from their meeting by an angry mob, which then set fire to the building and destroyed it.

17. By 1839 the executive committee of the Pennsylvania Anti-Slavery Society included women; (top left to right) Mary Grew, Abby Kimber, and Sarah Pugh; and (bottom left to right) Margaret Jones Burleigh and Lucretia Mott.

CHAPTER FIVE

WALKING WITH GOD

Let us not hesitate to be the Messiahs of our age.

—LUCRETIA MOTT

What pushes a silent, personal quest to grow into a movement? It is fitting that we step back for a moment to reflect on the message of faith that pervaded everything the abolitionist women sought to do. These early feminists were empowered by faith and a conviction that they were acting in the name of God. They were, in many respects, religious revolutionaries. Their vision, zeal, and love, plus their journey from domestic life to public stage, must be viewed in that light.

Perhaps the most underappreciated aspect of the origin of this form of modern feminism is its Christian roots. In past decades it has become common to see the feminist movement as secular. Bruised by centuries of subjugation in patriarchal institutions, with the church in the lead, many feminists believed secularism was the only path to freedom and equality.

It might be tempting, in light of this hardened attitude, to regard the Christianity practiced by early feminists as nothing more than convention, while promoting the narrative that in emancipation they began to shed their religious chains. But the true story of the abolitionist sisterhood leads us to a different conclusion altogether.

First expressing their Christian voice around the issue of slavery, women found a language in faith for their own emancipation. The plain message of the gospels gave clarity and purpose to the mission, yet brought the full wrath of the establishment church down upon these early feminists.

Imagine the courage it took to stand up against such a wall of resistance. Imagine the pain of devout women who were subjected to condemnation by the very ministers believed to be their moral leaders.

The ranks of abolitionist women were filled with devout Christian women inspired by the life of Christ. One after another they were struck hard by the terrible dissonance between their cherished Christian beliefs and the societal norms that supported the economy of their culture. As Angelina Grimké wrote in 1829, before she moved to the North from Charleston, "May it not be laid down as an axiom that that system must be radically wrong which can only be supported by transgressing the laws of God."[1] Thus, they defined their cause as holy.

We can bring these women's actions into sharp focus by exploring these religious roots—beginning with the question, how did it come to be that the church aligned itself with slaveholders?

IT WAS A sobering truth in the early nineteenth century that, not only did institutional religion support slavery, it was one of the cradles in which slavery rested and was nurtured. It was the Southern church that gave religious cover to slavery, citing carefully chosen Bible verses and propagating the notion that the slaves were heathens—an inferior race in need of control. Steeped in tradition and convention and ensconced in the economic comfort of a settled status quo, established Christianity blessed slavery in all its forms. This was not the revolutionary church of Jesus Christ, but the embedded church of a culture and economy that reinforced its well-being through a selective interpretation of the Bible.

For instance, it was often argued by slavery's supporters that Abraham had slaves. The Ten Commandments mentioned slaves twice. The apostle Paul admonished, "Slaves, be subject to your masters"—and he returned a runaway slave to his master. These biblical "proofs" were sought to justify slavery. And what of Jesus? Here it was not so much what he *said*—for he never spoke in support of slavery—but what he *didn't* say. An editorial in the *Richmond Enquirer* put it this way in 1820:

> If domestic slavery had been deemed by Jesus Christ the atrocious crime, which it is now represented to be, could it have been passed over without censure? Would the

doctrines of salvation have been illustrated by a reference to it, direct and unequivocal?—should we not have been told, not that the rich man, but that the slaveholders, could not enter the kingdom of heaven?

The arguments were meant to be soothingly persuasive to those who might feel a troubled conscience. Among the most common arguments was the claim that the slaves, once heathens in their native land, received religious instruction and found God in the benevolent paternalism of the slave plantation.

These ideas, often preached from the pulpit, were like a narcotic for the masses. As the pastors spoke, so the congregations believed. In that era, there was virtually no freedom of thought in the local church. Pastors were regarded as God's anointed representatives—not just teachers and guides, but the ultimate authorities on faith and practice. If a pastor stood before a congregation and declared something holy or sinful, it was so. In this way, the church sanctioned slavery.

Into this hypocrisy stormed the abolitionist women, who claimed not only a moral authority but also employed a theological brilliance worthy of St. Augustine to make their case.

In 1836 two documents written by the Grimké sisters shattered the long silence of Christians on the matter of slavery.

In writing her *Appeal to the Christian Women of the South*, Angelina believed that she could reach out to the women of her home—women who knew her. She wanted to express the love she had for her Christian sisters by offering them a new path. On many occasions, even knowing how Angelina's beliefs had changed, these sisters had remained her friends, disagreeing with her but trusting her faith was true. Now she asked them to take one more step. For those who didn't know *her*, she promised that she knew *them*, and had often prayed for their eyes to be opened. True morality, she assured them, laughed at the puny efforts of man to control it and it leaped all barriers, like a light bounding across the land. And since the Bible was the highest moral authority, she got down to the hard work of giving slavery a rigorous biblical test.

She challenged the argument that the great patriarchs of the Old Testament—foremost among them, Abraham—held slaves and therefore it was justified. "Do you really believe that patriarchal servitude was like American slavery?" she wrote. Biblically, she argued, Abraham's household was a loving mingling of family and servants, whom he trusted enough to arm, make them heirs, and give them religious training. "I admit that a species of *servitude* was permitted to the Jews," she wrote, "but in studying the subject I have been struck with wonder and admiration at perceiving how carefully the servant was guarded from violence, injustice and wrong." Indeed, their very status of servitude was different than the current slave population. Comparing the two, Angelina wondered, did American slaves sell themselves into slavery and receive the purchase money in their own hands? Did they become insolvent and offer themselves for servitude? Did they commit crimes for which they were delivered to servitude for restitution? No! None of these conditions applied.

Angelina dismantled, brick by brick, the argument that American slavery was somehow biblically sanctioned. Her most provocative argument came in discussing Jesus Christ and his golden rule. Addressing the frequently cited claim that Jesus surely would have condemned slavery if he had considered it immoral, she presented her strongest argument yet, one that would resonate and be repeated throughout the women's abolition movement:

> But did not Jesus condemn slavery? Let's examine some of his precepts. "Whatsoever ye would that men should do to you, do ye even so to them." Let every slaveholder apply those queries to his own heart; Am I willing to be a slave—Am I willing to see my mother as a slave, or my father, my sister, or my brother? If not, then in holding others as slaves, I am doing what I would not wish to be done to me or any relative I have; and thus have I broken this golden rule which was given me to walk by.[2]

Angelina's use of theology to address slavery was a call to action for her sisters in the South. Yes, she acknowledged, women might feel powerless to take action, but Angelina sought to inspire them with reminders of the courage of biblical women—and also presented contemporary evidence that women were empowered. Citing how women of the Anti-Slavery Society of Boston were mobbed and assaulted—and yet prevailed—she said that Southern women could do the same. Not just because it was the morally correct thing to do but because history itself was marching over and through them: "Can you not, my friends, understand the signs of the times; do you not see the sword of retributive justice hanging over the South, or are you still slumbering at your posts?"

The response to Angelina's appeal was immediate and harsh. As mentioned earlier, copies of it were burned by the postmaster when they arrived in Charleston, and a bounty put on her should she step foot in her home city.

But perhaps the most hurtful response to Angelina's appeal came not from the South but from another Quaker woman in the North. Catharine Beecher was an abolitionist but also a fierce advocate of women's "proper sphere" in society. She received Angelina's text and was urged to circulate it in the North. Instead, she sat down and penned a lengthy reply to Angelina. Men, she pointed out, were, by God's holy division, the actors in society; women were the subordinates who infused their domestic settings with warmth. This was not merely a social order but a *divine* one.

In Catharine's view, women were the silent forces in the domestic sphere, whose loving, peaceful presence, devoid of opinion, spread a perfume of goodness to the men and children in their circle—an influence that might act upon men to fight evil in the public arena and inspire children to grow into faithful citizens. In exchange, the chivalrous men protected and encouraged the maintenance of this loving spirit. As she wrote,

> Woman is to win every thing by peace and love; by making herself so much respected, esteemed and loved, that to yield to her opinions and to gratify her wishes, will be the free-will offering of the heart. But this is to be all ac-

complished in the domestic and social circle. . . . But the moment woman begins to feel the promptings of ambition, or the thirst for power, her aegis of defense is gone.

In a spirited exchange of letters, Angelina tried to convince Catharine that she was wrong to say it was God's will that women be relegated to a position of dependence and defenselessness. Her dismay and frustration were plainly felt in her sharp words:

I cannot refrain from pronouncing this sentiment as beneath the dignity of any woman who names the name of Christ. No woman, who understands her dignity as a moral, intellectual, and accountable being, cares aught for any attention or any protection, "vouchsafed by the promptings of chivalry, and the poetry of romantic gallantry." Such a one loathes such littleness, and turns with disgust from all such silly insipidities. Her noble nature is insulted by such paltry sickening adulation, and she will not stoop to drink the foul waters of so turbid a stream. If all this sinful foolery is to be withdrawn from our sex, with all my heart I say, the sooner the better. Yea, I say more, no woman who lives up to the true glory of her womanhood, will ever be treated with such practical contempt. Every man, when in the presence of true moral greatness, "will find an influence thrown around him," which will utterly forbid the exercise of "the poetry of romantic gallantry."[3]

In these letters, Angelina was evolving in her Christian thinking. It was not just the rights of the slave that consumed her but also the rights of women to fight on behalf of abolishing slavery. And her opponents in this mission were not just the men of the establishment but also the women who agreed with them and accepted their own subservience as God given.

LUCRETIA MOTT WAS one of the most eloquent and purposeful Christian spokeswomen. For her, the Quaker principle of the "inner light"—Christ's spirit within—guided her to trust her own sense of morality. If Christ was inside her, she could find her conscience there, not in the words of others.

"I know from blessed, heart-cheering experience the excellency of having a God to trust in seasons of trial and conflict," she said in a speech at the 1854 Women's Rights Convention in Philadelphia. In this spirit, she was able to resist interpretations of Christ's word by flawed religious men and instead proclaim,

> It is not Christianity, but priestcraft that has subjected women. Such dupes are men to custom that even servitude, the worst of ills, comes to be thought a good, till down from sire to son it is kept and guarded as a sacred thing. Women's existence is maintained by sufferance. The veneration of men has been misdirected, the pulpit has been prostituted, the Bible has been ill-used.[4]

Sarah Grimké, too, had much to say on this dangerous topic. More than her sister, Sarah struggled deeply with the tenets of the Quaker faith in making her case. Although, as a Quaker, an antislavery position was acceptable, as a *female* Quaker, she was bound by a separate code: to be quiet and obedient, not to express ego, or give way to the sin of pride by speaking in public. Praying for guidance, agonizing in the dark nights over her decision, she ultimately decided to take the antislavery case directly to the clergy. This was a much more shocking act than merely speaking to the public, for the Christian clergy were held above the common standard, and for a mere woman to challenge them was an unthinkable act.

Yet she did just that.

In *An Epistle to the Clergy of the Southern States*, Sarah asked, "[H]as not your interpretation of the Word of God induced thousands and tens of thousand to receive as truth, sanctioned by the authority of Heaven, the oft repeated declaration that slavery, American slavery, stamped as it is with all its infinity of horrors, bears upon it the signet of that God whose name is Love?"

Sarah went on to cite the core biblical passage of creation, where God makes man in his own image and gives him dominion over all living things. Slavery, she charged, has "wrested the scepter of dominion from his hand, slavery has seized with an iron grasp this God-like being, and torn the crown from his head. Slavery has disrobed him of royalty, put on him the collar and the chain, and trampled the image of God in the dust."

The inconsistency of theology is striking, she wrote: "How could God create man in his own image and then invest his fellow worms with power to blot him from the world of spirits and place him on a level with the brutes that perish!"[5]

These questions, asked one after the other, were the most cogently articulated critique of the church's inconsistency. And they had a dramatic impact. Thus stung, the clergy began to awake and take offense.

When Angelina and Sarah took their quest out of the world of letters and onto the public stage, the clergy was ready with a sharp defense. At Amesbury, Massachusetts, on July 17, 1837, months after the first Female Anti-Slavery Convention, Angelina argued with two local men about slavery in the Bible. This is considered to be the first public debate between the sexes in the United States.

Angelina expressed her dismay that "every minister in our land . . . will stand almost in a solid phalanx against woman's rights." Soon after her public debate, the Reverend Hubbard Winslow made a speech at the Bowdoin Street Church in Boston in which he claimed,

> The world has had enough of Fanny Wrights; whether they appear in the name of avowed infidelity, or of civil and human rights, or of political economy, or of morals and religion, their tendency is ultimately the same—the alienation of the sexes, the subversion of the distinguishing excellence and benign influence of women in society, the destruction of the domestic constitution, the prostration of all decency and order, the reign of wild anarchy and shameless vice.

Reference to Scottish abolitionist Fanny Wright was, of course, meant to inflame. In the 1820s Wright was a controversial and profane voice in the public discussion of morality and faith, calling religion "the perverter of human virtue," and advocating for free love. Her radical views would not have sat well with the abolitionist women, not to mention the public at large, and by making the comparison Reverend Winslow was committing an incendiary act. Wright's name alone might be viewed as a slanderous linkage—that women who spoke out were sexually immoral, atheist, and even crazy.

Angelina responded to this tirade by saying, "I am glad H. Winslow of Boston has come out so boldly and told us just what I believe is in the hearts of thousands of men in our land. I must confess my womanhood is insulted, my moral feelings outraged."[6]

Six weeks after the first Female Anti-Slavery Convention, the clergy struck back again, this time with an organized condemnation of the women who were so boldly speaking out in the public square. Congregational ministers in New England assigned one of their own, the Reverend Nehemiah Adams (often called "South-side Adams" because of his support of the South), to pen "The Pastoral Letter of the General Association of Congregational Ministers of Massachusetts," which was read from the pulpits and published on June 28, 1837 in the *New England Spectator*. Without mentioning names, it was clear that the Grimké sisters were its chief targets. The letter presented itself as an important message to the faithful, bearing upon the "cause of Christ." Without mentioning slavery specifically, the letter left no doubt that the clergy felt their position had been insulted and even usurped by those who would introduce an unseemly debate upon their congregations. It was the pastoral influence not the ravings of zealots that must be respected, they argued— and they must have known this would carry weight within their congregations because, as they reminded the faithful, their ministers were "ordained of God" to be their teachers and guides. This closed system, which the women were daring to question, provided a seemingly airtight way to reinforce principles which they deemed to be godly—end of discussion. How it must have rankled them to find these obstinate *female* voices raised against them. And it was the women to whom the pastoral letter delivered its harshest rebuke:

> We invite your attention to the dangers which at present seem to threaten the female character with wide spread and permanent injury. The appropriate duties and influence of women are clearly stated in the New Testament. Those duties and that influence are unobtrusive and private, but the sources of mighty power. When the mild, dependent, softening influence of woman upon the sternness of man's opinions is fully exercised, society feels the effects of it in a thousand forms.
>
> The power of woman is in her dependence, flowing from the consciousness of that weakness which God has given her for her protection and which keeps her in those departments of life that form the character of individuals and of the nation. There are social influences which females use in promoting piety and the great objects of Christian benevolence, which we cannot too highly commend. . . .
>
> But when she assumes the place and tone of a man as a public reformer, our care and protection of her seem unnecessary, we put ourselves in self defence against her, she yields the power which God has given her for protection, and her character becomes unnatural.

The letter posed a vivid image in its argument for women's dependence, comparing women to vines: "If the vine, whose strength and beauty is to lean upon the trellis work and half conceal its clusters, thinks to assume the independence and the overshadowing nature of the elm, it will not only cease to bear fruit, but fall in shame and dishonor into the dust." In other words, if the vines (women) overgrew the elm (men), the elm would shrivel and die.

The Grimkés, for their part, were not intimidated, even publishing a response of their own in the *New England Spectator* under Sarah's name, entitled "Letters on the Equality of the Sexes and the Condition of Women." Citing the passage referring to the threat to the female character, she wrote,

> I rejoice that they have called the attention of my sex to this subject, because I believe if woman investigates it, she will soon discover that danger is impending, though from a totally different source that that which the Association apprehends,—danger from those who, having long held the reins of usurped authority, are unwilling to permit us to fill that sphere which God created us to move in, and who have entered into league to crush the immortal mind of woman. I rejoice, because I am persuaded that the rights of woman, like the rights of slaves, need only be examined to be understood and asserted, even by some of those, who are now endeavoring to smother the irrepressible desire for mental and spiritual freedom which glows in the breast of many, who hardly dare to speak their sentiments.

Once again, Sarah Grimké relied on the words of Jesus, not those of the male clergy, pointing out that in the Sermon on the Mount, when Jesus set forth the duties of his followers, he never differentiated by sex or by class. She challenged anyone to show where Jesus gave different directions to men and women, therefore showing it to be a distinction wholly crafted by men who could not accept the truth that men and women were created equal as moral and accountable beings, and that what was right for men was also right for women.

Almost teasingly, Sarah referred to the characterization of women's weakness, writing, "If physical weakness is alluded to, I cheerfully concede the superiority; if brute force is what my brethren are claiming, I am willing to let them have all the honor they desire; but if they mean to intimate that mental or moral weakness belongs to woman, more than to man, I utterly disclaim the charge."

The idea of caring paternalism did not sit right with Sarah, who rejected this false protection of her weak womanhood. As she put it, "The motto of woman, when she is engaged in the great work of public reformation should be, 'The Lord is my light and my salvation; whom shall I fear? The Lord is the strength of my life; of whom shall I be afraid?'" She concluded, "Ah! how many of my sex feel in the dominion, thus unrighteously exercised over them, under the gentle appellation of protection, that what they have leaned upon has proved a broken reed at best, and oft a spear."

Perhaps there was a more subversive strategy at play when the clergy attacked outspoken abolitionist women.

Being without credible defense in their support of slavery, they turned on the messengers, hoping the sight of women storming into the public square would so outrage the population that their ideas would be lost in the outcry.

AS ARGUED EARLIER, were it not for the Second Great Awakening, abolitionist feminism might not have flourished. With its message that God dwells within the individual, the Second Great Awakening loosened the rigid formulas of faith and spiritual practice, opening the door to inner questioning. In the words of the early feminists, we find the flowering of this relational theology, the natural enemy of restrictive hierarchies.

Nineteenth-century feminism was founded on the belief that women's activism was God's work. Yet this aspect of mainstream US feminism was lost in the next century. Why was feminism later secular when it was birthed and nurtured in devotional circles?

In part, it was because, while the message of Jesus was radicalizing for many women, the organization of Christianity (i.e., the church) was patriarchal and its attitudes about women's role archaic. Would-be Christian feminists were forced to bring into alignment two opposing forces—the word of God, which inspired and elevated them, and the dictates of the church, which harkened back to the cult of true womanhood preached in the early nineteenth century. Many women could not find a bridge between these two realities, and decided that to be pure feminists meant rejecting the patriarchy of organized religion.

Contemporary historians have minimized, and in some cases omitted, the religious core of feminism. But even a cursory survey of the writings of early US feminists reveals the primacy of their faith. Take, for instance, Lydia Maria Child's opening statement at the 1837 convention: "[I]t is the duty of every human being to labor to preserve, and to restore to all who are deprived of it, God's gift of freedom; thus showing love and gratitude to the Great Redeemer by treading in His steps." At the 1837 convention, the women claimed equality for themselves, using the same theological assumptions that motivated them to claim it for the slaves. While this put them in direct opposition to the prevailing religious dogmas of the day, they insisted they were on a sacred mission, and it was their deep, passionate faith that fueled their revolutionary social activism.

These early feminist women recognized something that has often been ignored. That is, Christianity and feminism were both revolutions, founded on the same core principle—that every person has equal value in the eyes of God. They found their strength, purpose, and courage in their faith; the words of that great revolutionary Jesus Christ spoke to them in every moment.

For the abolitionist feminists, faith was a living, breathing reality. Belief in God's calling made them determined to change what was wrong. Their faith gave them the power to think for themselves and to act. For them faith was not an impediment to engagement but a moral basis for their actions. They felt secure in their testimony because it grew from their deepest beliefs. Their calling was "the cause of God, who made mankind free, and of

Christ, who died to redeem them from every yoke." The call from God superseded all else and compelled them to throw off the restrictions against their sex. It was their duty, as much as men's, "to plead the cause of the oppressed" so that all could live in freedom.[7]

Each woman resolved to do "all that she can by her voice, her pen, and her purse" regardless of the "perverted application of Scripture" that had become ingrained in the culture. These women had found a faith liberated from patriarchal institutions. Theirs was an un-churched piety. It was both a bold and humble faith. Even as they rebelled against prevailing theology, they scheduled "appointed seasons for prayer" throughout their organizing efforts. The Quakers would sit in silence, listening for God's voice. In one instance, Sarah Douglass recorded the transformation she experienced when sitting with her sisters: "My heart acknowledged the superior eloquence of silence—the beauty of sitting down in humility and heartbrokenness to wait the operation of the Holy Spirit—and then to feel its gentle influence distilling like dew upon the soul."[8]

Leaning on God gave them courage to lift their voices in truth telling, regardless of the consequences. Abby Kelley, who would become one of the most acclaimed public speakers of her time, claimed it was God who gave her eloquence, through "the still small voice within, which may not be withstood, that bids me open my mouth."[9]

Angelina expressed her faith in action, stating, "I desire to talk but little about religion, for words are empty sounds, but may my life be a living epistle known and read of all men."[10]

The congruence of faith and feminism was experienced by these women. These early feminists show us an inspirational example of the power of Christianity to open the heart, comfort the mind, and give both courage and sustenance even in the darkest days. Judgment, hatred, pride, and envy fell away in the practice of feminist Christianity. Love triumphed. Not the chained love of the diminished and dependent, but the fully expressed love of the equal—which was, in its essence, the love preached by Jesus Christ. In this sense, both Christianity and feminism were transformative movements, bearing the same message.

In an address later published in the *Liberator* on July 21, 1832, Sarah Douglass wrote of her reliance on God, "I know from blessed, heart-cheering experience the excellency of having a God to trust to in seasons of trial and conflict." This "excellency," their belief in something both universal and bigger than any one individual, gave the abolitionist women the courage to challenge the clergy and their dogma. They accepted unequivocally the harmony of their faith and feminism. Their "holy duty" included changing the messages that emanated from America's pulpits in order to end the subjugation of slaves and women.

We can revive the holy alliance of faith and feminism in today's activism. It begins with the understanding that the religious roots of feminism are part of our sacred tradition. For abolitionist feminist foremothers, faith was the fuel for their activism—and this is equally true of the leaders of other great movements, from Martin Luther King Jr. to Gandhi. In these cases, faith drew the movements toward peace, empathy, and brotherly-sisterly love—away from anger, revenge, and recrimination. Feminism can draw from the power of faith while pulling religion away from patriarchal practices and polarizing ideologies. Furthermore, religion calls feminists to be intersectional—constantly searching, redefining oneself in ever more inclusive contexts, always relying on the fundamental precept to love one another and to cherish each other's diverse experiences.

In the late 1800s the British suffragist Maude Royden would put the conflict between religion and feminism into a new context, writing, "I discount the easy but deceptive retort that 'organised religion' is always conservative, for one has only to look at this history of Christianity to see that organised religion has often been a revolutionary force in order to realize that it may easily become so again."[11] Looking beyond structures, man-made and imperfect, to the vital message of Christianity, allows us to find both feminists and people of faith occupying the same radical center.

CHAPTER SIX
SYMPATHY FOR THE WOMAN

We hold these truths to be self-evident:
That all men and women are created equal.

—ELIZABETH CADY STANTON

Returning to Lynn, Massachusetts, after the 1838 convention, where she had dared to create public declarations as a mob raged outside, Abby Kelley was determined to renew her commitment to the abolitionist cause. But now the cause had expanded beyond the emancipation of the slaves to embrace her own and other women's emancipation. The burning of Pennsylvania Hall was not a challenge to abolition; it was the backlash against women assuming the right to a public voice. The crowds were incensed by the sight of women, black and white, walking together. Even the press coverage of the event focused on the "scandalous" acts of women, barely mentioning their cause.

Given that these sentiments existed within the abolitionist movement as well, Abby wanted to bridge what had once been an impossible divide. Maybe it was time for the female antislavery societies to begin collaborating with men for the larger purpose. But not all women agreed. Lucretia Mott, in particular, believed that by operating independently, women amassed greater power and independence. But many women shared Abby's growing conviction that men and women must unite their resources and power. Abby chose William Lloyd Garrison's New England Anti-Slavery Society as the place to start.

Garrison was open to women's participation, but while they were welcome at the society's meetings, they could not become members. Abby learned that change was in the air: she attended the next meeting to hear a resolution raised that all *persons* who shared antislavery principles be invited to join as members. After heated debate, the resolution passed! Abby was among the first to enroll. As a single woman and only twenty-seven, she overcame her shyness and was the first to take the floor and speak. She was then appointed to a three-person committee assigned to create a document—an "Appeal to New England Clergy"—to speak out against slavery.

Her appointment so offended the traditionalists in the society that some of them, including several clergymen, stormed out of the meeting and vowed to leave the organization. The president asked Abby to resign. Momentarily intimidated, she agreed, but then, as if shaking herself from a stupor of subservience, she changed her mind and remained on the committee.

The next day, her outraged detractors continued to try to unseat her. When that effort failed, they presented a motion to abandon the committee altogether. Eventually, that motion failed as well, but not without a long and angry debate.

Ignoring the critics, Abby and her committee wrote the appeal only to find that many clerical bodies refused to even read it, given a woman's participation in the writing.

After the convention, Abby returned to Lynn and resumed teaching, but she was a changed woman. She could not forget the discrimination she experienced. She envisioned embarking on the public lecture circuit to help awaken the culture to this irrational prejudice against women.

This idea now had special urgency because the Grimké sisters, the standard bearers on the lecture circuit, had retired to private life. After the 1838 convention, Angelina and Theodore had moved to Fort Lee, New Jersey, and Sarah lived with them. They were pouring themselves into writing a book, *American Slavery as It Is: Testimony of a Thousand Witnesses*. It was a historically significant assimilation of first-person accounts by former Southerners and other social analysts and observers, in addition to the press. They wrote not only of the suffering of the slaves but also of the tormented consciences of many slaveholders, and the broken, inhumane culture that allowed these conditions to exist. The facade of gentility was exposed, laid bare in their writing—designed, according to Angelina, "to show the awful havoc which arbitrary power makes in human hearts and to incite a holy indignation against an institution which degrades the *oppressor* as well as the oppressed." While widely read and circulated, *American Slavery as It Is* took an emotional toll on Angelina and Sarah. "It cost us more agony of soul to write these testimonies than anything we ever did," Angelina admitted.[1] For this and other reasons, the sisters became more reclusive.

But Abby continued to correspond with Angelina, Sarah, and Theodore, seeking their guidance about her proposal to begin a lecture tour. In January 1839, she wrote an anguished letter to Theodore, pouring out her fears and sense of inadequacy:

> I have nothing to start upon, no name, no reputation, no scrip, neither money in my purse. What is the greatest is the feeling of my own inability for the work. I have not the gift. How can I make bricks without straw? Had I the qualifications of Sarah or Angelina, I could not wait another day.[2]

Theodore and the sisters sent back letters of support. Abby was also fortified by this passage from Corinthians 1:27: "But God chose the foolish things of the world to shame the wise; God chose the weak things of the world to shame the strong." She wrote, "How true it is that all great reforms have been carried forward by despised and weak means. The talent, the learning, the wealth, the church and the state, are pledged to the support of slavery. I will go out among the honest-hearted common people, into the highways and byways, and cry, 'Pity the poor slave!'" And so she did, beginning in Connecticut where she traveled across the state, her lectures gaining momentum as the sisterhood gathered behind her to organize meetings.

Receiving word that Abby was starting her tour, Sarah Grimké wrote to her, "I am glad to find that thou were not dismayed by the opposition. What thou hast done will do more toward establishing the rights of women on this point . . . than a dozen books." Lydia Maria Child also urged her on, after hearing Abby speak. "I wanted to thank you for your spirited conduct on that occasion. . . . I have no doubt that great good was done."[3]

Across the Northeast, the women who had dedicated themselves to the abolitionist cause were experiencing a moment of truth. Like Abby, others were beginning to question the cultural roles of the sexes. As the date of the third Convention of the Female Anti-Slavery Society approached, there was an uneasy stirring in the ranks.

ON AN AFTERNOON in late April 1839, Mayor John Swift paid a visit to Lucretia Mott at her Philadelphia home. They greeted one another politely but cautiously. Nearly a year had passed since their last encounter on the eve of the destruction of Pennsylvania Hall. Lucretia knew that Swift was no friend of the slave, nor of the women who championed the slaves' cause. But his chief concern, on the eve of the third Female Anti-Slavery Convention, was to avoid the violence of the previous year.

It had been a difficult convention to organize. The women found themselves split over the need for a female society. Lydia Maria Child wrote to Lucretia that their conventions "always seemed to me like half a pair of scissors."[4]

Abby also wrote to Lucretia, expressing her growing sense that men and women must work together, "promiscuously," not separately, to which Lucretia responded with an impassioned letter:

> I should be very glad if women generally and men too, could so lose sight of distinctions of sex as to act in public meetings, on the enlightened and true ground of Christian equality. But that they cannot yet do this is abundantly evinced by the proceedings of your New England Convention last spring. . . . It is already acknowledged that our Conventions have done something towards bringing woman to a higher estimate of her powers— and it will be a subject of regret if those who are qualified to enlighten others, and who may be instrumental in removing the prejudice by which so many are bound, should hastily withdraw and leave their sisters "to serve alone."
>
> I would therefore . . . [seek to] persuade thee . . . to suspend the conclusions to which your arguments are leading you, in order that you may give us your company this spring, when we may examine the whole ground more fully.[5]

Not persuaded, Abby informed Lucretia that she would not attend, choosing instead to go to the American Anti-Slavery Society Convention in New York. The Grimkés would not be present either, as Angelina's pregnancy prevented travel.

Then there was the question of locale. Not surprisingly, most venues in Philadelphia were against the idea of hosting the women, unwilling to risk the fate of Pennsylvania Hall. The women finally settled on the Pennsylvania Riding School, a barnlike structure on Filbert Street, and a date was set for May 1, 1839. More than one hundred women signed up to be there.

Now Mayor Swift nervously questioned Lucretia about the plans. As she would later describe to her sisters, he inquired where the convention would be held, if it would be confined to women, if to only white or white and black women, if they would be "parading the streets" together, if the meetings would be held only in the daytime, and how long they would continue. He suggested that the meeting be held in Clarkson Hall, which was already guarded by his officers, that they should not meet in the evening, and particularly that they should avoid walking publicly with black people.

Lucretia replied that Clarkson Hall was not large enough for the gathering, and they would meet at the Pennsylvania Riding School, which was, "to the shame of Philadelphia," the only building they could procure of sufficient size. She assured him that there would not be evening meetings, for the Riding School had only a barn roof and no ceiling, making lighting difficult. She also told him that the ladies had never "paraded the streets" with black people, but merely walked as the occasion demanded and would do so again. On this principle, there was no compromise. Indeed, they were expecting black women to attend, and they would be accompanied to the meetings.

The mayor was still uneasy, and thus assured Lucretia that he would have officers ready for their protection— even though she told him they were not needed.

So the convention began, and on the first day Mayor Swift sent a messenger to find out exactly when the convention would end, as he had officers waiting. Lucretia responded that she could not tell when their business would be finished, but in any case, she had not asked for his aid. Ignoring this distraction, the women turned their attention to the business of the convention, with new voices and old raised to offer resolutions affirming their sacred mission.

There was a notable sophistication in this third meeting, an effort to address not just the overt evils of slavery but the need to elevate and care for the free black population as well. The first resolution spoke of the difficulty in finding teachers for black children's Sunday schools, and urged all members who had a hand in employment to do their best to remedy the situation:

> Resolved: That henceforth we will increase our efforts to improve the condition of our free colored population, by giving them mechanical, literary, and religious instruction, and assisting to establish them in trades, and such other employments as are now denied them on account of their color.

The resolution was seconded by Clarissa C. Lawrence, a black woman who had been vice president of the all-black Salem Female Anti-Slavery Society before it joined with white women. She gave a stirring statement:

> We meet the monster prejudice everywhere. . . . It kills its thousands every day; it follows us everywhere, even to

the grave; but, blessed be God it stops there. You must pray it down. Faith and prayer will do wonders in the anti-slavery cause. Place yourselves, dear friends, in our stead. We are blamed for not filling useful places in society; but give us light, give us learning, and see then what places we can occupy. Go on, I entreat you. A brighter day is dawning. I bless God that the young are interested in this cause.

Once again, the women called out the clergy for its un-Christian stance, noting that the clergy was

ingenious in devising terms of reproach, and assailing with ridicule the women engaged in this cause. They can plead for the heathen in China, and describe a terrestrial paradise in Liberia, but do all in their power to retard us in our work. Not content with passing by the poor slave themselves, they would prevent us from extending to him the light of the gospel. The excommunication of devoted Christians from the church, etc., are but a development of their hostility to the holy cause of good will toward man, without regard to color. It is this inconsistency which we regret—it is this spirit which we are called upon to meet, and against which, upon all proper opportunities, we should bear our testimony.[6]

There was unity in this meeting, and determination. It was unanimously decided to convene a fourth convention in Boston in 1840. However, that convention would never take place. By then, the original movement had evolved; there was division in individual societies, and leaders like Mott were invited to join forces with the male societies. The work continued—but in a different form.

The most important product of the third convention was a document entitled *An Appeal to American Women on Prejudice against Color*, which, in part, read,

> Women of America! we entreat you to ponder these things in your hearts; to consider how far you are "guilty concerning your brother." It is in your power, to roll back this tide of cruel prejudice, which overwhelms thousands of our fellow creatures, equally gifted with ourselves by our common Father, though ruthlessly robbed of their heritage. . . .
>
> Endeavoring to apply this rule, we call, on behalf of our colored sister, for an equal participation with yourselves, in every social advantage, moral, literary and religious; assured that as we conscientiously tread the path of our duty the difficulties will disappear, and we shall each be able to say in the words of a celebrated writer, "That power which has swept from my heart the dust of prejudice, has taught me also to respect excellence wherever found."[7]

MEANWHILE, ABBY WAS on fire, touring and speaking. She fiercely promoted the fundamental idea of sympathy for the slave, while also drawing a connection with women's social oppression:

> If you could imagine a colored man's feelings when kept at bay by his white brother, then you can have some faint conception of a woman's heart, when she awakes to a sense of her true position as a responsible being and sees herself fenced in by the iron prejudices of centuries.[8]

Abby's impassioned words were a clarion call to the antislavery societies, and many charged her with inciting the argument that ultimately tore them in two. The poet John Greenleaf Whittier called her "the bombshell that exploded the [American Anti-Slavery] society."[9] A few decades later, writer Phebe Hanaford said, "Abby Kelley Foster is one of the noble reformers of our century. . . . [Had she] lived in the days of martyrdom, she would doubtless have been burnt at the stake: as it is, the martyr spirit she has exhibited will crown her among American women, when their right to the ballot is conceded."[10]

The bitter dispute came to a head in Massachusetts, where Garrison's acolytes waged a struggle with a newly organized contingent of traditionalists, who appeared as wolves in sheep's clothing to upend progress.

In sum, Garrison's followers represented the radical core of abolitionism, which promoted dignity for all persons, including women. They were opposed by traditionalists, including many religious conservatives who sought "practical" solutions to slavery. They isolated it from other social or moral questions, and were especially opposed to women's rights. They were open segregationists, able to carve out a small piece of indignation for the plight of the slave, while turning a deaf ear to other inequalities. This conflict, which began in the male antislavery societies, spread to the female organizations, particularly in Massachusetts, where Garrison had his strongest support. Attending the Boston Female Anti-Slavery meetings, Maria Weston Chapman noticed an invasion of new members with strong anti-Garrison views. Soon conflict rocked what had once been a united organization. In what appeared to be a fraudulent election, a spate of anti-Garrison female officers were seated, and they quickly called for the dissolution of the organization.

The pro-clergy, anti-women's-rights contingent quickly reorganized themselves as the Massachusetts Female Emancipation Society, while the pro-Garrison members reinstated the Female Anti-Slavery Society, now hobbled by the shocking split.

The power of the female antislavery societies would never be restored to its diverse, interdependent, mutually respectful *sisterly* beauty. Many hearts were heavy, knowing there would never again be a convention of antislavery women. But dawning was a new era that held promise as well as dissent. For in standing their ground and insisting on their own rights, along with the rights of the slaves, women like Kelley and Mott were beginning to give birth to a wider vision that would forever change the course of history for women, and for all humankind.

The most promising development was the decision of the American Anti-Slavery Society to allow women to join its contingent as delegates at the 1840 World's Anti-Slavery Convention in London. Eight women were chosen to travel to London, among them Lucretia and Mary Grew. It was with a great deal of excitement that these two friends packed their trunks and boarded the ship. The voyage across the Atlantic was long, but they sensed the historic nature of what they were doing. But their dreams were stymied when the world organization rejected the American idea of seating women in its midst.

In fact, to their astonishment, the main business of the convention was, not slavery, but women's right to participate in the meeting. Even before their arrival, groups of clergy and their supporters had been lobbying against giving women a voice or a role. Back and forth the men went, in passionate speeches, both for and against the women's right to be seated officially at the meeting.

It must have been painful for Mary to see her own father, Henry Grew, a delegate from Philadelphia, rise and speak against the participation of women, using God to justify his voice as well as the silencing of hers: "The reception of women as a part of this Convention would, in the view of many, be not only a violation of the customs of England, but of the ordinance of Almighty God, who has a right to appoint our services to His sovereign will."[11]

By the end of the day, the men decided female delegates could not be admitted as convention members, but would be allowed to sit in the balcony behind a screen, where they could look on in silence. Stunned by this outcome, the women argued that the billing of the meeting was that it was a *world* convention. And they were part of the world. The only reply was that the wording had just been "poetical license."

Garrison had not been present that first day, his ship being delayed at sea. When he arrived to learn the women had been excluded, he refused to take his seat but joined them in the gallery, where he sat silently for the entire convention. Later he would write, "With a young woman placed on the throne of Great Britain, will the philanthropists of that country presume to object to the female delegates from the United States, as members of the convention, on the ground of their sex? In what assembly, however august or select, is that almost peerless woman, LUCRETIA MOTT, not qualified to take an equal part?"[12] The decision, nevertheless, was firm.

Mary Grew, speaking of the reaction of the attendees toward the women's delegation, said, "[We are] regarded as quite a phenomenon, which everyone is anxious to see. We are, almost every day, introduced to numbers of persons who request this *privilege*, and who look upon us with countenances of mingled astonishment and respect."[13]

Also in attendance, sitting on the sidelines, was Elizabeth Cady Stanton. Her new husband, Henry, had agreed they both should go to London for their honeymoon to attend the convention.

Elizabeth was the well-educated daughter of a lawyer in Johnstown, New York, whose long perusals in her father's law library as a young girl sparked her interest in the need for women's rights. Like Angelina, she insisted on removing the word "obey" from her wedding vows. Her marriage to Henry, who, while an abolitionist, was not particularly sympathetic to women's rights, placed her in the company of women who would nurture her emerging passion. Watching the vote to exclude women, she observed, "It struck me as very remarkable that abolitionists, who felt so keenly the wrongs of the slave, should be so oblivious to the equal wrongs of their own mothers, wives and sisters." She also noted, with a stab at wry humor, "The clerical portion of the Convention was most violent in its opposition. The clergymen seemed to have God and his angels especially in their care and keeping, and were in agony lest the women should do or say something to shock the heavenly hosts."

Excluded from the main business of the convention, Lucretia and Elizabeth soon began to talk. Elizabeth was elated by her new friendship. "These were the first women I had ever met who believed in the equality of the sexes," she wrote. "The acquaintance of Lucretia Mott, who was a broad, liberal thinker on politics, religion, and all questions of reform, opened to me a new world of thinking."[14]

Soon, the business of the convention hardly mattered to the women as they pursued their underground plotting. Walking arm in arm along the streets of London, Elizabeth and Lucretia began to plan a future gathering of their own, which would be a women's rights convention. It was an ambitious project, but they knew somehow it would come to pass.

Once Mary and Lucretia returned to America, they looked for every opportunity to encourage women to develop their talents and capabilities. Mary wrote in one of her annual reports, "It is a satisfaction to believe that by the concentration of our efforts . . . we not only advance the cause of the slave, but that the fettered mind of woman is fast releasing itself from the thralldom in which long existing custom has bound it, and by the exercise of her talents in the cause of the oppressed her intellectual as well as moral being is raised into new life."[15]

These abolitionist feminists realized that their own ability to advocate for the rights of all was greatly diminished by sexism. For Mary, Lucretia, and women like them, working for women's rights was a way they themselves could become empowered, conscious, and healed.

AFTER THE CONVENTION that had so invigorated her,

Elizabeth returned with Henry to begin their life together, not yet certain of her course of action. The following years would be both joyful and frustrating, as Henry pursued a law degree and she had four children (she would ultimately have seven). Moving to the distant town of Seneca Falls, New York, in 1846, Elizabeth felt her spirit ebbing out of her. Only thirty-one, she grew depressed and lonely, missing the exuberance of urban life. Suddenly she saw with new eyes the debilitating plight of women, who were chained to their homes and children, deprived of the light of intellect and collegiality, as their husbands traveled freely in the public sphere. For this reason, she cherished any opportunity to be with Lucretia, who, although the mother of four (and now a grandmother), had never ceased her vibrant public life.

In 1848 she was thrilled to receive a communication from Lucretia, saying she planned to visit Elizabeth while she was in the area to meet with members of the Seneca Nation. Indeed, Lucretia spent a full month with the Senecas, inspired by the way the women engaged fully in decision making. She recounted sitting at the table with them, noting how much freer they were in their clothing, untethered by corsets and weighty skirts. She saw them speak openly and learned how revered they were. She noticed the men did not regard women as property; in fact, the communities were very hard on men who treated their wives poorly. In her own reading, Elizabeth marveled that Native American women seemed more free and powerful than their white sisters. They became an impactful model for Elizabeth, which she brought to a tea party arranged by Lucretia. Relieved and pleased to be in the company of the woman who understood her so well and shared her passion, Elizabeth spoke of her discontent, and the urgent feeling that they must do something—and do it now. Astounding as it may seem, the women decided then and there that they would organize a convention for women's rights, in five days' time, while Lucretia was still in the area. As Elizabeth recalled the momentous occasion,

> I poured out, that day, the torrent of my long-accumulating discontent, with such vehemence and indignation that I stirred myself, as well as the rest of the party, to do and dare anything. My discontent, according to Emerson, must have been healthy, for it moved us all to prompt action, and we decided, then and there, to call a "Woman's Rights Convention." We wrote the call that evening and published it in the Seneca County Courier the next day, the 14th of July, 1848, giving only five days' notice, as the convention was to be held on the 19th and 20th.[16]

Lucretia then sought out her old friends Thomas and Mary Anne McClintock, wealthy abolitionist philanthropists who lived in nearby Waterloo, to help them plan, and a second tea was hastily arranged at the McClintock home to discuss the format of the convention. During the discussion, someone came up with the idea of modeling their manifesto on the Declaration of Independence—complete with a statement of equality and a list of grievances patterned on the Declaration's list against King George III.

The Woman's Rights Convention of Seneca Falls was the first meeting of its kind in the United States, and it was called on impulse, at a tea party, by a handful of women who had been trained in the ranks of abolitionism. It was the second tea party that would change the course of American history.

In spite of the short notice, two hundred women convened at the Wesleyan Chapel on July 19. Elizabeth read the Preamble: "We hold these truths to be self-evident: that all men *and women* are created equal; that they are endowed by their Creator with certain inalienable rights . . ." Then she read the Declaration of Sentiments and Grievances, which she had drafted over the previous few days, detailing the injustices suffered by the women of the nation.

ON THE SECOND day of the convention, men were invited to attend, and forty did, including the famous African American abolitionist Frederick Douglass. That day, the convention passed twelve resolutions calling for specific equal rights for women. Only one of these met with controversy—the call for the right to vote—although it ultimately passed. This resolution, which signaled the beginning of the women's suffrage movement, would be a tinderbox for controversy lasting seventy-two years.

The convention fully woke Elizabeth from her isolating depression, giving her new motivation for her tireless work on behalf of women's rights. Her speeches and writings revealed a brilliant mind and a gift for words that managed to reach the heart of every matter. She was especially eloquent on women's place in the natural universe, exalting their God-given rights. As she wrote after the convention,

Among the many important questions which have been brought before the public, there is none that more vitally affects the whole human family than that which is technically termed Woman's rights. Every allusion to the degraded and inferior position occupied by women all over the world, has ever been met by scorn and abuse. From the man of highest mental cultivation, to the most degraded wretch who staggers in the streets do we hear ridicule and coarse jests, freely bestowed upon those who dare assert that woman stands by the side of man—his equal, placed here by her God to enjoy with him the beautiful earth, which is her home as it is his—having the same sense of right and wrong and looking to the same Being for guidance and support. So long has man exercised a tyranny over her, injurious to himself and benumbing to her faculties, that but few can nerve themselves against the storm, and so long has the chain been about her that however galling it may be she knows not there is a remedy.[7]

Lucretia too felt new purpose in the expansion of the mission. It was like a release from chains that had held even women like herself back for too long. She wrote in "Discourse on Women" that woman "has so long been subject to the disabilities and restrictions, with which her progress has been embarrassed, that she has become enervated, her mind to some extent paralyzed; and, like those still more degraded by personal bondage, she hugs her chains."

Women may have hugged their chains in the past, but a new freedom now emerged. With the end of the Seneca

Falls Convention, and as the word spread, they had tasted the wine of liberty and authority. And they would never go back.

In her 1855 letter to Elizabeth Cady Stanton, Lucretia emphasized the convention of 1837 as the true catalyzing agent that led to women obtaining equal rights:

> From the time of the 1st Convention of Women—in New Y[ork] 1837—the battle began. A resolution was there warmly discussed & at length adopted by a majority— many members dissenting, "that it was time that woman should move in the sphere Providence assigned her, & no longer rest satisfied in the limits which corrupt custom & a perverted application of the Scriptures had placed her."

Although Lucretia and Elizabeth might have told the story differently—Lucretia citing the 1837 convention and Elizabeth citing Seneca Falls—perhaps the truth lies in a different calculation. Seneca Falls represented not a beginning but the first official, visible, and public flowering of the pursuit of women's rights. Yet it would not have come to pass were the ground not sown by the Female Anti-Slavery Convention of 1837. It was, after all, Lucretia and others, who had developed a set of organizing principles, that persuaded Elizabeth that such a convention was possible in 1848. And while Seneca Falls was, as it billed itself, "The First Convention Ever Called to Discuss the Civil and Political Rights of Women," some of the vital essence of 1837 was missing. In particular, the importance of interracial organizing was abandoned in 1848; only one black participant attended—Frederick

Douglass. Without the presence of black women, the vision of the convention was effectively middle class and white. Post–Seneca Falls feminists did not have the language to talk about race, and as the suffragist movement grew, it often pitted women's rights against black rights; many feminists, including Stanton herself, voiced the opinion that black men should not have the right to vote until white women did. Contrast that with the 1837 women, who elevated the notion of "sympathy," not only for the slave but for each other across racial lines. Interracial organizing was a radical act on the part of the 1837 women that wasn't fully appreciated at the time and is only beginning to be acknowledged now. By recognizing the 1837 convention as the true birthplace of American feminism, we also embrace the diverse roots of the feminist movement.

CHAPTER SEVEN

A BODYGUARD OF HEARTS

When the true history of the antislavery cause shall be written, women will occupy a large space in its pages; for the cause of the slave has been peculiarly woman's cause. Her heart and her conscious have supplied in large degree its motive and mainspring. Her skill, industry, patience, and perseverance have been wonderfully manifest in every trial hour.

—FREDERICK DOUGLASS

A special solidarity followed the abolitionist feminists throughout their lives. The successes they achieved were made possible by the strength of their relationships. These women loved each other deeply, and the richness of their friendships gave them an elevated level of support. As Angelina once put it, "I feel that when I am speaking, I am surrounded by a bodyguard of hearts, faithful and true."[1]

As we follow our band of sisters into their later years, we find they remained loyal to each other, in sickness and health, in disappointment and progress. Individually and together, they continued their work for the emancipation of slaves and women, always buttressed by their relationships with each other, from which they drew strength and sustenance. This was the most consistent theme of their lives, even as their circumstances and even commitments changed.

Abby Kelley's decision to take on a public role, difficult at first, in time became as natural to her as breathing. In 1845 she married Stephen Foster, a devoted abolitionist, and their marriage was a truly modern one—equally bound in the joint causes of abolition and women's emancipation. When she gave birth to a daughter, Alla, Abby declared that motherhood would not sidetrack her from her mission. She continued touring and speaking. "When I left my little daughter," she wrote, "I felt as though I should die. But I have done it for the sake of the mothers whose babies are sold away from them." Indeed, as Alla herself noted after Abby's death,

> When asked how she could bear to leave her little daughter, she would reply, "I leave my child in wise and loving hands, and but for a little, while the slave mothers daily have their daughters torn from their arms forever and sold into torture and infamy." Never was a mother more devoted, more self-sacrificing than she. Had she been less noble, less brave, less tender of her child, she would have remained at home to enjoy her motherhood at the expense of other mothers. She once exclaimed, "The most precious legacy I can leave my child is a free country!"[2]

Abby's gift was an intuitive ability to relate to those she served in her advocacy. As she noted,

> It is not my vocation to string together brilliant sentences or beautiful words. My mission has been back among the people, among the hills and the hamlets, and I have had no weapon but the gospel truth in its simplicity. . . . All the great family of mankind are bound up in one bundle. When we aim a blow at our neighbor's rights, our own are by the same blow destroyed. Can we look upon the wrongs of millions—can we see their flow of tears and grief and blood, and not feel our hearts drawn out in sympathy?[3]

Abby's articles and speeches were often published in the *Liberator*. An editor was known to have said, "This extraordinary young woman unites a power of intellect that is exceedingly rare and an eloquence that nothing but flint can withstand."[4] Abby supported other papers, such as the *National Anti-Slavery Standard*, a paper that had replaced the *Emancipator* as the organ of the American Anti-Slavery Society. She regularly sent them reports of her meetings in Lynn, Massachusetts, along with open letters responding to political events. When the *National Anti-Slavery Standard* needed a strong editor, she knew just the person for the job—her colleague, Lydia Maria Child.

Maria's once-prolific writing career had been brought to a standstill after she embraced the abolitionist cause. Her contemporary, Phebe Hanaford, spoke of how Maria's dedication to abolition hurt her success as a writer: "Lydia Maria Child was one of those philanthropists whose able pen won others to the advocacy of freedom. . . . The exercise of this noble spirit caused her books to fall into sudden obscurity." Hanaford went on to say, "[I]f her pen would but record her reminiscences of those days, it would command an army of readers."[5] Now Abby wanted to find a way to restore Maria's voice to the public sphere.

When she first approached Maria about becoming editor of the *Standard,* Maria hesitated, not sure that she was up for the job. But Abby insisted. "You are just the editor we want. We need oil upon the waves. . . . [W]e have had too much of fighting. There is now an opening for something better."[6]

Maria accepted the job and moved to New York, her husband coming along to support the effort. But almost immediately, problems surfaced. Maria's executive committee gave her conflicting criticism of her editorial style: "One complaining that I don't put in editorial enough!! Another that I write about subjects not strictly antislavery; . . . another that I neglect non-resistance and women's rights, another that I don't quote more of Garrison." To Maria's dismay, her greatest critic was the one person she had expected to be her biggest ally—Abby.

Maria's instinct was to make the *Standard* a first-rate paper and set a warm, embracing tone. She wanted to develop the paper as a forum for multiple viewpoints and a magnet to draw in new abolitionists. Abby, however, wanted the *Standard* to take the same uncompromising positions she did. She saw it as a weapon against slaveholders. To Maria, Abby's standpoint was that "every person who is not an outspoken and out-acting abolitionist

. . . is a dangerous member of the community." In contrast, Maria wanted to avoid "fighting and controversy," and sought to "confine myself to appeals to reason and good feeling; that I should aim more at *reaching the people* than at pleasing abolitionists." Both women dug in their heels.

Abby had developed a "teetotal pledge," which required abolitionists to withdraw from churches and political parties if those organizations did not publicly take an antislavery stance. She felt it was "the greatest aid of any measure I have ever adopted, in producing agitation," and she wanted Maria to promote it in the *Standard*. Flatly refusing, Maria said the pledge was "utterly *sectarian* in its character. To push everybody off the anti-slavery platform who will not leave their religious associations seems to me narrow and proscriptive. I resist their effort to coerce the free will of individuals." Resigning from the paper, Maria announced that she would be involved in the abolitionist movement "in my own way, according to the light that is in me."[7]

This argument between Abby and Maria reflects the growing pains typical of movements, where a shared vision does not necessarily translate into a pure alignment of attitudes and actions. Maria believed in the cause, but she sought to temper the stridency often used by others and instead appeal to a broader, more conservative audience. Rather than alienate those unprepared to fully accept freedom for slaves—not to mention women's rights—she strove to make the *Standard* a more welcoming vehicle. Abby's all-or-nothing approach offended her. She thought it would drive away more people than it would bring into the fold, and so she resigned. And although Maria would never again be involved in organized action, she continued to write about the forces of oppression—against African Americans, Native Americans, and women—as she promised, in her own way.

In 1860, for instance, Child was commissioned to write the preface to Harriet Jacobs's autobiography, *Incidents in the Life of a Slave Girl*, and helped edit the manuscript. Jacobs's autobiography was written, in part, to appeal to white women in the North by demonstrating the humanity of black women and their shared roles as mothers. Alongside tales of Jacobs's escape and attempts to free her children, *Incidents* discusses her desperation to avoid rape at the hands of her master—including his threats to sell her children if she did not capitulate to his desires—proving that slave women were trapped in an impossible power struggle and not to be blamed for their sexual abuse. Her book remains an integral piece of American literature.

Sadly, the interracial roots of the women's movement faltered. By midcentury, Abby found herself frequently having to explain to those who joined the women's rights movement just how significant its beginnings were in women's antislavery organizing. Upon hearing a disparaging comment about the abolitionist women at the 1851 Worcester Women's Rights Convention, she replied, "For fourteen years I have advocated this cause by my daily life. Bloody feet, Sisters, have worn smooth the path by which you have come up hither."[8]

SARAH AND ANGELINA Grimké seldom made public

statements in their later years, but their early messages endured. Their spiritual lives, which once gave them the moral clarity to move out into the world as prophets and activists, now burned more gently but were still alive. In her letter "Equality for the Sexes," Sarah spoke for both sisters when she said, "Let us keep in mind that no abolition is of any value which is not accompanied with deep heart felt repentance." They believed that the social change to which they devoted their lives would occur only with the inner transformation of the human heart. In this idea they were prescient, for even after slavery was abolished, the Jim Crow era—with its heavy hand of discrimination and violence toward black people—demonstrated that morality could not be legislated. People must *believe* in equality for it to flourish. In its purest form, "repentance" meant *accepting* racial equality, not just reluctantly adhering to the force of law. It meant extending black brothers and sisters the hand of friendship and attempting to make up for the grievous acts against them throughout America's history. But this repentance was not easily found; it remains a profound issue to this day.

Like many of their sisters, the Grimkés easily made the transition from abolition to feminism, in their later years becoming dedicated suffragists. In fact, one of Sarah's final acts, at the age of seventy-nine, was to claim the right to vote in a most dramatic way. On March 7, 1870, Sarah and Angelina set out in a heavy snowstorm to the local polling place. There, along with forty-two other women, they cast ballots and placed them in a box set up specifically for women's votes. A raucous crowd followed them, but their taunting did nothing to dissuade the sisters, who had been hearing such disparagement throughout their lives. It would be fifty more years before women in America won the right to vote.

The Grimkés and Sarah Douglass maintained a close relationship over the years. After Grace Douglass died in 1842, Sarah devoted the rest of her life to the cause of educating young women. Her girls' school in Philadelphia became a model for the times, melding the joint causes of racial and gender equality. Sarah taught her girls more than reading, writing, and sewing; she also taught them chemistry, biology, and geology.

In 1853 Sarah merged her girls' school with the Quaker-founded Philadelphia Institute of Colored Youth. She taught there for the next twenty-five years. Curious about the new sciences, she studied both anatomy and physiology at the Female Medical College of Pennsylvania. She lectured publicly on the female body, making her one of the first female educators to empower young women with basic knowledge of their own bodies. The first issue of the *Weekly Anglo-African* in 1859 highlighted her lectures: "[They] breathed throughout recognition of the God whose handiwork they presented to the view. They were not mere details of scientific facts, but were enriched by numerous and beautiful illustrations, well calculated to elevate the mind, and so practical as to engage the attention of many on whom theories, however grand and inspiring, are lost."

In a speech published in the *Liberator* on July 21, 1832, Sarah expressed what inspired her and her mother to become social activists. She spoke first of sympathy: "We must feel deeply before we can act rightly; from that absorbing, heart-rending compassion for ourselves springs a deeper sympathy for others." And then she spoke of her complete reliance on God: "I know from blessed, heart-cheering experience the excellency of having a God to trust to in seasons of trial and conflict. What but this can support us?" The Douglass women were inspired by a vital relationship with God that sustained them in their work toward justice.

This faith was present for Sarah when her mother passed away: "[Y]et God did so comfort me even while my fingers sewed the cap that was to cover her precious head as she lay in her coffin that I could have sung aloud as he sweetly whispered in the ear of my soul. 'Beauty shall spring out of ashes and life out of the dust.' He will comfort thee!"[9]

An activist even into her later years, Sarah worked to raise funds to support Frederick Douglass's abolitionist newspaper, the *North Star.* She advised her cousin Joseph C. Bustill to become an agent for the paper. In 1849 she helped organize the all-black Women's Association of Philadelphia, with the goal of supporting Douglass's cry for black nationalism. In spite of these examples of her strategic community organizing, she would have wanted to be remembered as a teacher. On July 23, 1859, the *Weekly Anglo-African* summed up her career: "Mrs. Douglass has been long known, both in New York and Philadelphia, as a most successful and self-sacrificing teacher. Many of our most honored wives and mothers owe their intelligence to her faithful instructions."

Sarah felt her passion for education was a sacred calling. When she was seventy, Sarah rose up indignantly upon hearing how a former student characterized her as "dragging out a miserable existence." She bristled in her response:

O said I eagerly, how she is mistaken! A miserable existence indeed! When I am doing the will of God concerning me! Doing the work I love; doing it with all my heart and soul and mind and strength! Finding my rich reward is on high. I have thoroughly enjoyed teaching this autumn and winter. Going out morning by morning, leaning on the strong arm of my invisible friend and reaching my schoolroom with thanksgivings and praises in my heart and on my lips.[10]

Even after Sarah Grimké died in 1873, Sarah Douglass continued to correspond with Angelina and Theodore Weld and their son, Charles. In a letter to Charles Weld, we meet the aging Sarah Douglass:

Oh, dear Charley, what a comfort your letters would be to me if I could only read them! I have to study over your letter in order to find out all about Mr. Garrison. . . . I suffer greatly from rheumatism, cannot do any house work not even sweep a room. Yet I go to school every day because my bread depends on it. I ride part of the way because it is so difficult for me to walk. I enjoy being in school. I love my work, God wills me to do it. It is sweet work.[11]

In 1898, sixteen years after Sarah Douglass's death, a group of citizens wrote "A Tribute of Respect to the Veteran Teacher." In it, they referred to her as "one who has long and faithfully served in the elevation and culture of a race and as a pioneer of education among her people."[12]

LUCRETIA MOTT AND Mary Grew were joined in revolutionary spirit for the remainder of their lives. The bond these Philadelphia women shared transcended the organizations of their early days. Though they were of different religious traditions, their common foundation was an abiding faith in God's true word. Raised a Baptist, Mary later joined the Unitarian church, which was more aligned with her progressive views. She and Lucretia had only disdain for ministers who gave biblical arguments supporting slavery. One minister wrote, "As it appears to us too clear to admit of either denial or doubt, that the scriptures do sanction slaveholding . . . to declare it to be a heinous crime is a direct impeachment of the word of God."[13]

In contrast to this minister, Mary and Lucretia used their faith not to rationalize injustice but to open their hearts to greater sympathy for those around them, even slaveholders. Both the Unitarian and the Hicksite Quaker faiths supported social action. Mary shared Lucretia's disillusionment with hierarchical, rule-oriented, institutionalized religion. She wanted to practice a more egalitarian faith, one in which authority rested in the personal experience. As these women were beginning to develop more trust in their own inner wisdom, they sought out religious forums that were less dogmatic and where they were welcome to fully participate.

Mary's life commitments can be seen in her role as one of the editors of the antislavery paper the *Pennsylvania Freeman*. Founded in 1836 by pioneering abolitionist

Benjamin Lundy, the *Freeman* was adopted as the official paper of the Philadelphia Anti-Slavery Society in 1837 and tackled a variety of peace and justice issues. Mary was one of the editors from 1845 to 1850. As editor, Mary promoted international peace. She took a stand against the Mexican-American War, which was fought to gain control of Texas. Mary felt—as did Lundy and other abolitionists—that the Mexican-American War was a conspiracy by Southern slaveholders to "[furnish] facilities to men to enslave their brethren!" Mary also endorsed other reform movements, including the "redemption" of prostitutes, prison reform, and the eradication of capital punishment. With the bold, honest wielding of her pen—one of the only forms of power for women at the time—Mary exposed her readers to ways they could make a difference in the world. She used the written word to provoke an apathetic public to action.[14]

In many ways Lucretia and Mary symbolized the bridge between abolitionism and the women's rights movement. They moved from one to the other seamlessly because equality was the basis for both. They were regular attendees and leaders of women's rights meetings. In 1852 they cochaired a regional convention in West Chester, Pennsylvania. In the keynote address, Lucretia once again made the connection between the oppression of women and the oppression of slaves when she said,

Woman is told that the fault is in herself, in too willingly submitting to her inferior condition, but like the slave, she is pressed down by laws in the making of which she has no voice, and crushed by customs that have grown out of such laws. She can not rise therefore, while thus trampled in the dust.[15]

Staying active throughout their lives, Mary and Lucretia participated in the Fifth National Women's Rights Convention in Philadelphia. Mary was appointed to the business committee and Lucretia was one of the vice presidents. Years later, in 1870, Mary became president of the Pennsylvania Woman Suffrage Association. She called the meeting to order with these words:

> We are not well known in this community, as this is our first public meeting. . . . We appeal to the American nation . . . to put into practice the political doctrines they hold, those doctrines which every American especially and particularly glories in . . . that "taxation without representation is tyranny." . . . Our effort is solely to put the ballot into the hands of women."[16]

In 1871 Mary was asked to speak at a meeting of the Radical Club of Chestnut Street in Boston. It was an organization of progressive religious thinkers. "Essential Christianity" was the theme of her speech. In it, she insisted that no philosopher or metaphysician had ever devised a system of ethics equal to that of Jesus's teachings: "Whatsoever you would that men should do to you, do ye even so unto them." A central theme of her remarks was mutual respect and universal equality. John Greenleaf Whittier sent this poetic tribute to the meeting:

[Mary] in her gracious womanhood
She gave her days to doing good.
She dared the scornful laugh of men,
The howling mob, the slanderer's pen.
She did the work she found to do,—
A Christian heroine, Mary Grew!

. . . .

The way to make the world anew,
Is just to grow—as Mary Grew![17]

After all the antislavery work she instigated and ac-
complished, Lucretia went on to make other significant
contributions. She fought for the rights of Native Americans, helped to establish Swarthmore College in 1864,
and became president of the American Equal Rights
Association. Her work had lasting significance and her
words are still called upon and revered today.

In 1880 their mutual friend Sarah Pugh wrote Mary to
tell her that Lucretia was gravely ill. Mary wrote Lucretia
a final letter:

My Beloved & Revered Friend,

It may be that I shall no more see your face and hear
your voice, before you enter the celestial city and I meet
you there. Therefore I want to thank you, before you go,
for all that you have been to me: for all the blessedness
which has flowed from your soul into my soul, from your
life into my life. . . .

Thy affectionate friend of many years,
Mary

Mary's life was even more radical than those of her fellow abolitionist and feminist sisters, in that she lived in a same-sex relationship. Mary and her lifelong friend and constant companion, Margaret Burleigh, lived together, and Margaret accompanied Mary when she traveled, whether it was on vacation or to various antislavery and women's rights meetings. Women in same-sex relationships at that time were especially isolated. In response to a letter of condolence following the death of Margaret in 1892, Mary wrote to a close friend:

> Your words respecting my beloved friend touch me deeply. Evidently . . . you comprehend and appreciate, as few persons do . . . the nature of the relation which existed, which exists, between her and myself. . . . To me it seems to have been a closer union than that of most marriages. We know there have been other such between two men and also between two women. And why should there not be. Love is spiritual, only passion is sexual.[18]

Mary would die within a year of Margaret's death.

LUCRETIA'S DEAR FRIEND and sister in revolution, Elizabeth Cady Stanton, became a public force after Seneca Falls. With Lucretia, Lucy Stone, and Susan B. Anthony, she organized the American Equal Rights Association to align the women's rights movement with the drive for black suffrage. When this organization collapsed at the passage of the Fourteenth Amendment, Elizabeth and Susan founded a boldly radical feminist newspaper called the *Revolution*, for which Stanton wrote many articles calling for women's control over their own persons in marital relations; liberalized divorce laws that would recognize marriage as a legal contract like other contracts; radical improvement of prisons, poor houses, and insane asylums; and an end to state-authorized prostitution. Using the newspaper as a launching pad, Elizabeth and Susan founded the National Woman Suffrage Association.

Later still, Elizabeth proposed a third party to represent labor and women's interests. Far ahead of her own time, she held that such a third party should push for infant day-care centers for working mothers as part of the public school system, free school lunches, public colleges for working-class youth, abolition of capital punishment, an end to police brutality, and equal justice in the courts for the poor and the rich.

Elizabeth could not have fully appreciated how dramatic bringing Susan B. Anthony into the feminist cause would be. Susan was a true radical who preached radical acts: "You cannot keep the good will and win the good votes of all the good men of all the good parties of the State by allying yourselves with one or the other or all of them!" she preached. "You must stand as disfranchised citizens—outlaws—shut out of the body politic, humble supplicants, veriest beggars at the feet of all men of all parties alike."[19]

Among Susan's most revolutionary acts was voting in the 1872 presidential election in her hometown of Rochester, New York. Along with fourteen others, Susan had registered to vote, but when she showed up at her polling place she was questioned before being allowed to cast a ballot. The polling inspector asked her under oath if she was a United States citizen. Yes. Did she live in the district? Yes. Had she accepted bribes for her vote? No. Since she answered all the questions properly, she was allowed to cast her vote for president and members of Congress.

But a poll watcher launched a complaint, and nine days later Susan was arrested. (Initially, the other fourteen women were arrested as well, but only Susan was prosecuted.) She was indicted and brought to trial in June 1873, before a jury of twelve men. However, in the course of the trial the judge determined that the case was so clear-cut—women did not have the right to vote—that a jury verdict would be unnecessary, and she was declared guilty.

The judge then turned to Susan and asked if she had anything to say as to why the sentence of the court should not be pronounced upon her.

"Yes, your honor," she answered, "I have many things to say. My every right, constitutional, civil, political and judicial has been tramped upon. I have not only had no jury of my peers, but I have had no jury at all."

The judge bristled. "Sit down, Miss Anthony. I cannot allow you to argue the question."

"I shall not sit down," Susan replied. "I will not lose my only chance to speak."

"You have been tried, Miss Anthony, by the forms of law, and my decision has been rendered by law."

Susan said, "Yes, but laws made by men, under a government of men, interpreted by men and for the benefit of men. The only chance women have for justice in this country is to violate the law, as I have done, and as I shall continue to do." She pounded her hand loudly on the table.

> Does your honor suppose that we obeyed the infamous fugitive slave law which forbade to give a cup of cold water to a slave fleeing from his master? I tell you we did not obey it; we fed him and clothed him, and sent him on his way to Canada. So shall we trample all unjust laws under foot. I do not ask the clemency of the court. I came into it to get justice, having failed in this, I demand the full rigors of the law.

With no further discussion, the judge issued a $100 fine and court costs. When Susan said she had no money to pay the fine, the judge could have committed her until it was paid, but he chose not to do so. Small victories.

Susan B. Anthony would become the most famous feminist of the times. When she died in 1906, her eulogy was delivered by a female pastor, the Reverend Anna Howard Shaw. The reverend's words might have referred to any of the early feminists, whose sacrificial acts paved the way for a change they themselves would not experience.

> She did not gain the little bit of freedom for herself, but there is scarcely a civilized land, not even our own, in which she has not been instrumental in securing for some woman that to which our leader did not attain. She did not reach the goal, but all along the weary years what marvelous achievements, what countless victories! The whole progress has been a triumphal march, marked by sorrow and hardship, but never by despair. The heart sometimes longed for sympathy and the way was long, and oh! so lonely; but every step was marked by some evidence of progress, some wrong righted, some

right established. We have followed her leadership until we stand upon the mount of vision where she today leaves us.[20]

Those beautiful words resonate down through the century to our own time: "The heart sometimes longed for sympathy, and the way was long, and oh! so lonely." For a time the relational ethos that gave abolitionist women such courage and power dissipated under the force of the backlash. The sewing circles, petition drives, and conventions no longer united the women of the movement in a singular purpose. With the end of slavery, the feminists turned their attention to the suffragist cause.

New female voices gained prominence during that time—women like Sojourner Truth, whose personal story and gift for oratory cut to the heart of the quest for women's equality. Born into slavery, and having experienced firsthand the struggle of her people, Truth was able to articulate better than most the dimensions of the challenge women were now facing. For while black women fought alongside their brothers to achieve abolition, once it happened their brothers did not reach back to make sure the rights extended to them as well. "There is a great stir about colored men getting their rights," she noted in 1867, "but not a word about the colored women; and if colored men get their rights, and colored women not theirs, the colored men will be masters over the women and it will be just as bad as it was before."[21] In "Ain't I a Woman," her most famous speech, Truth used her own history as a slave to prove that, given the opportunity or necessity, women can do what men can do, bringing to light, much as Harriet Jacobs did before her, that the definition of womanhood conveyed by white Northerners excluded black women.

Other women emerged to carry on the fight—women like Ida B. Wells, Alice Paul, Mary Church Terrell, Dorothy Day, Jeannette Rankin, Margaret Sanger, Mary Ann Shadd Cary, and others, who labored into the twentieth century, finally securing the right to vote. Down through the century, other women stepped forth, their names imprinted on the tapestry of feminist action—women like Bella Abzug, bell hooks, Gloria Steinem, Paule Marshall, Wilma Mankiller, Angela Davis, Pauli Murray, Audre Lorde, Alice Walker, Anita Hill, and the members of the Combahee River Collective. Progress was slow; rights secured did not guarantee equality of the heart. More than a century after the abolitionist women first declared that a woman's place was in the public sphere, Betty Friedan sent shock waves through the social order by declaring just that in *The Feminine Mystique*.

The 1960s ushered in what was termed the "second wave" of feminism, as women found themselves embracing the larger cultural and social revolutions of their time. More women than ever were entering the workplace and achieving independence. They were demanding the same rights as men, and equal pay, and they achieved a modicum of equal rights by law when the Civil Rights Act of 1964 included a provision prohibiting sexual discrimination by employers. The National Organization for Women (NOW) was founded and began campaigning for an Equal Rights Amendment (ERA). The ERA passed Congress on March 22, 1972, simply stating, "Equality of rights under the law shall not be denied or abridged by the United States or by any State on account of sex." It then began a six-year state-by-state journey to ratification. Almost immediately, thirty states ratified the amendment, but then progress slowed down. By the 1979 deadline, the ERA was three states short of the thirty-eight it needed for passage.

The failure of the ERA was due to many factors, including a strong conservative backlash. A variation of the cult of true womanhood was revived and preached by women like Phyllis Schlafly,[22] who successfully led the movement to halt the ERA in the 1970s. In fact, her organization's acronym, STOP ERA, stood for Stop Taking Our Privileges. Gloria Steinem, testifying before Congress about the ERA in 1970, drew a parallel between white women and black people. "Both suffered from such restricting social myths as: smaller brains, passive natures, inability to govern themselves (and certainly not white men), sex objects only, childlike natures, special skills, and the like. When evaluating a general statement about women, it might be valuable to substitute 'black people' for 'women'—just to test the prejudice at work."[23]

To this day, the central arguments of equality and human dignity rage on in the political sphere, corporate boardrooms, universities, and the media. Each legal step toward equity is combatted by a ferocious backlash. Now, 180 years after the first convention of American women, we still fight for equality—in our paychecks, our sexuality, and our representation in the seats of power. Issues reflect the cultural struggles of the era, the glass ceiling, date rape, sexual harassment, and human rights for women and children across the globe. "Third wave" feminism has emerged on a broader plane seeking intersectionality among all groups: gender, race, class, religion, and sexual identity. Just as the abolitionist feminists found that seeking freedom and equality for black people opened up a pathway to their own quest for equality, today's feminists see their cause in a more expansive framework. The principle is clear: if some are oppressed, all are oppressed. Thus marriage equality becomes a feminist issue. Black lives matter becomes a feminist issue. Poverty becomes a feminist issue.

The early abolitionist women carried the burden of passing the torch, and now it belongs to us, in this new world we inhabit. As the Reverend Anna Howard Shaw further proclaimed, in a nod to the future, "The promised land lies just before us. It is for us to go forward and take possession."

"THINE IN THE BONDS OF WOMANHOOD"

*In the different voice of women lies the truth of
an ethic of care, the tie between relationship and
responsibility, and the origins of aggression in the
failure of connection.*

—CAROL GILLIGAN

In 1978, I earned my masters in counseling at Southern Methodist University. Looking back, it seemed as if most of my life prepared me to heal fractures and restore connections—beginning with my own recovery of self. I met Harville Hendrix, a psychologist and professor of religion, a year after my divorce, and we began dating. We were both emerging, bruised and quite wary, from our first marriages. In one of our first conversations I asked him, "If you could wave a magic wand, what would you like to do with your life?" He wanted to write a book about why couples fight. He sensed there was something profound in figuring out that common trauma, and he was right. He had a vision of healthy relationships that was enormously compelling, especially to me who believed in their significance, and the caring that comes from real connection. I soon proposed.

Over the next three decades, our marriage became a living laboratory that spawned Imago, couples therapy focused on the relationship rather than the individuals. We drew from feminist relational theory, including the groundbreaking work of Jean Baker Miller, Carol Gilligan, and the pioneering psychologists who founded the Stone Center. These women married feminism with Freud, augmenting his insights about the unconscious and correcting some of his blind spots around male supremacy and sexual abuse. We were able to face our childhood wounds, trace how that pain created an unconscious image of the person we would be drawn to, and finally to consciously strengthen the way we relate to one another. I just made it sound easy, but for the two of us, each very stubborn, it was hard to put into practice. Two decades into our marriage we were on the brink of divorce (so much so that one of our counselors referred to us as the couple from hell), and we nearly abandoned not just each other but the technology we had developed for relating across difference.

We have always supported each other's work behind the scenes, but in public it looked as if Harville focused on couples and I focused on the women's movement. These seemingly parallel tracks have always been intertwined and, in recent years, we are overtly working together to offer a new social structure: We believe that healthy relationships are the glue that holds, not just couples or families, but the world together. Relationships—love, connection, empathy, care, being understood, and the willingness to understand—are the up-river solution that can help heal so much of the down-river cleanup our society is currently focused on.

The urgency of building healthy relationships—between child and parent, spouses, neighbors, and citizens—is an ever-present reality for me. I never doubt that when Harville and I work together, it is very sacred work. We share the conviction of the mystic and philosopher Martin Buber, who posited that God resides in the between—in a relationship where two people hold one another in truest mutual regard. Both feminism and Imago are aligned in lifting up the banner of relationality. When couples engage in a dialogue, they begin to develop an empathic attunement that moves them into an egalitarian partnership and helps eradicate the old dominator/ subordinated model. In that way, Imago is eroding the patriarchy one couple at a time. This is a powerful healing energy that can happen right in our own homes—and how crucial it is that we heal, both as people and as a nation.

As I write these words, the country is reeling from the 2016 presidential election. We remain in mourning over the killing of multiple unarmed black people by the police, the killing of police officers in my hometown of Dallas, and the reemergence of terrorizing imagery, such as swastikas and nooses, scrawled on buildings. On a daily basis, people speak of feeling unsafe, silenced, devalued, scapegoated, and resentful. The relational science that can help shift any two people from conflict to connection in a precise way must be on the agenda—learned, focused on, practiced, and writ large—because a respectful relationship is the prerequisite for achieving liberty, equality, and justice for all. I say this with urgency now, but the abolitionist feminists said this, too. Elizabeth Margaret Chandler encouraged those early feminists to use their weekly sewing circles to "practice sympathy for the slave," meditating not on pity for "the less fortunate" but trying to imagine what it would feel like to be enslaved. She and others introduced the concept of what I would call "relational organizing" in their case organizing *with*, not on behalf of African Americans—and identified the racial prejudice even within the abolitionist movement as one of "the chief pillars of American slavery."

Nearly two hundred years later, breakthroughs in neuroscience have led to the discovery of neuroplasticity, or the fact that our brains can evolve, confirming what Chandler knew—that we *can* change what we think and feel. Moreover, we have social brains that are experience dependent. You can actually practice empathy, you can practice being curious rather than judgmental and critical, and you can practice equality. You may not be able to control your first reaction to a person, incident, or comment; but you can control your second and third. And all this work eventually helps to repattern your brain. You can practice skills that transform conflict and suspicion to connection and openness. What is being transformed is nothing less than the "white-supremacist capitalist patriarchy," as bell hooks calls it. In this love-driven relational approach, the dominator/subordinated dynamic of the patriarchy gives way to mutuality, equality, care, and collaboration. Finally, the building of healthy relationships becomes possible.

But how does this relate to the most pressing demands of our current political realities? What I've learned from the abolitionist feminists is that you can practice growing in yourself the capacity to coexist *in a movement* with people who think differently than you, that other people are simply that—other, not you. Once you recognize the otherness or difference of another, it's time to become curious about it. Over time, you can learn to honor that otherness, find opportunities for cooperation and collaboration, and heal the pain of disconnection. You can listen and be listened to. You can grow a healthy and affirmative movement composed of people who are not exactly like you.

PROGRESS IS MESSY, poignant, nonlinear. The abolitionist feminists woke up, individually and in small conversations, to the moral needs of their era. A collective consciousness took time to form. One spoke, then another, and another still—their ideals and longings pouring out in letters to each other, expanding the circle, eventually building a movement. In spite of the ways the conveners of 1837 advanced their cause, they did not achieve an end to slavery, which didn't occur until nearly thirty years after their historic meetings. Nor did the abolitionist feminists secure any new rights on behalf of women in general. The flurry of laws provoked by this first wave of feminism did not help most of the women you've met in these pages; most died before women had the right to own property, divorce, or vote, and before slavery was abolished. Still, this was a historic series of events organized by the abolitionist feminists, and the women involved knew that. Given the backlash they inspired, including the burning of their meeting hall, they were doubly convinced their actions were revolutionary.

But the most violent response, in its way, was that the radical, inclusive, interracial organizing history of these activists was buried, as was their Christian zeal, beneath a storyline that elevated two heroic white figures—Susan B. Anthony and Elizabeth Cady Stanton—as the creators of the women's movement. If the Seneca Falls Conference was the beginning of feminism in the United States, then the whole story is one where black men and white women were pitted against each other in the battle for rights afforded to citizens, and seemingly only one group could prevail. That story doesn't acknowledge the particular situation of black women as figures who embody each group's oppression. The story of the women's movement from Seneca Falls sets us up to see splits and rivalries as inevitable.

The second wave of US feminism in the late 1960s and '70s suffered from the inevitability of splits, too. It was grounded in sisterhood, as women met around their kitchen tables, told their stories, shared their pain, and made their plans. We called that connecting "consciousness raising"—helping us understand the systems of oppression in which we existed and thought of as "just life." The sharing of what had been secrets—sexual assault, body confusion, fear of ambition, shame about money or lack thereof—provided relief and invited others to tell the truth about their experiences. In many cases, political theory was drawn from the collaborative knowledge that if something was happening to so many women, perhaps its cause was political and cultural, not a personal failing, and its solution political as well. We learned to trust in one another—compassion, understanding, listening, validation—as the early feminists did. In small circles, we lifted up one another's voice.

The politics of the time, however, quickly split into factions, and dissociated from dialogue and validation. The sins and denial of our earliest breaths as a nation haunted the women's liberation movement. The early 1970s witnessed the emergence of a series of divisions within the women's movement: black and white, gay and straight, and splits along class, ability, and regional lines. Simultaneously, there was a powerful backlash akin to the "fifty years of ridicule," as Shulamith Firestone named the patriarchal reaction to the first wave.

During the backlash, black feminists regrouped and created many of the theories and practices we now accept as the gold standard of feminist discourse and action, both in the academy and in the trenches. For example, intersectionality (theorized by Kimberlé Crenshaw in 1989), the reproductive justice framework (imagined in 2003 by Loretta Ross, Toni Bond, and several other women of color), the through line from plantation to prison industrial complex (as identified by Angela Davis and Michelle Alexander in the twenty-first century), and the wide-ranging political theory of bell hooks. Despite the profound influence of black intellectual production driving contemporary feminisms, white women remain its most visible and valued spokespeople—another vestige of unfinished work when it comes to racial equality.

WHEN I DISCOVERED the small booklet detailing the first US feminist convention of 1837 on a dusty shelf in the Barnard library, it felt like an excavation—of self, to be sure, but also of our shared feminist history. Here was evidence of women, feminists, who saw the moral conflicts of their time in a way that was broad, inclusive, and visionary even for ours. The booklet became not so much an artifact of the past as a living, breathing portal into my own time. It introduced me to a remarkable group of women who spoke with voices still very much alive. Not only did I admire them, I wanted to be like them. To respond to the urgent demands of my era with the same resolve, dignity, and courage they brought to theirs, and to do so intersectionally and inclusively.

Learning of these early feminists, I began to feel an angst in my body that was decades—or centuries—old. I never understood where this sense of dread or unease came from. My family was odd, but it wasn't like I had such a bad life. We were materially resourced beyond most and I loved my sisters June and Swanee dearly. With the pamphlet and knowledge of these early feminists, though, I was given an assignment: *Feel this disturbance, understand it, and figure out what to do with it.*

I've come to see that many of the early feminists were catalyzed into action because they were experiencing a profound cultural dislocation, one that I had known both as a well-off woman teaching very poor children and as a female child in an extremely patriarchal family. The great rhetorical idealism expressed by our founding fathers in the democratic revolution had no business describing a nation that contained slavery. The words and actions of the abolitionist feminists enhanced my comprehension that we are a country founded on denial and dissociation as much as democracy. After all, twelve of our first eighteen presidents owned slaves, even as they intoned the most beautiful and soaring language of liberty. Everyone in the US has experienced (and been diminished by) this painful conflict. We have never fully faced, much less made redress for, our treatment of black people in this country. Still, a few women nearly two hundred years ago, both black and white, were able to pierce the denial in part because they were also excluded from the American promise that "all are created equal."

Powerfully, too, it was also because of the example of Jesus Christ—a man who did not dissociate from anyone—that these women were able to find a model for healing and radical change. Women, irrespective of race, were laughed at when they claimed any rights. The power their Christian beliefs had to motivate extremely bold behavior in the face of total ridicule struck me as a missing link—a key, even—in the story of early feminism in the United States.

It wasn't the only key, to be sure, nor the first one to be purposefully lost. As I discovered these women, I became aware, too, of the groundbreaking work of historian Sally Roesch Wagner, who helped recover the links between the creation of first wave feminism's goals and the Haudenosaunee (Iroquois) women. These tribal women, who shared geography with Elizabeth Cady Stanton and Matilda Joslyn Gage, inspired both the notion of votes for women and dress reform, as Native American women chose their chief and dressed in the loose pants and tunic style that Amelia Bloomer later popularized. I had also read the powerful words of Laguna Pueblo and Sioux author and scholar Paula Gunn Allen, who instructed us to look to indigenous communities to understand that societies without patriarchy and misogyny have indeed existed, and even coexisted with ours. Our history with indigenous people is another critical relationship that must be faced.

Still, this Christian key opened up thinking that enabled me to see how the organizing practices of the abolitionist feminists could be a blueprint for our current movement. I have identified seven spirited practices from their recovered movement to offer as a blessing and a path for feminists today.

ONE: Think and organize relationally

Unlike freedom, which can be the political achievement of the separate individual, equality is by nature a social construct that intrinsically involves connection and empathy. The abolitionist feminists did not know they were pioneers in the relational sciences I've spent my adult life studying and fostering, but their methods foretold our modern awakening to dialogue, safe conversation, and active listening—all told, a new way of being with one another. Relational communication is a technology, and one that fosters equality; a process that structures egalitarianism and give and take.

The women abolitionists attended to their friendships. They depended on their relationships for support. They maintained extensive correspondence, looked after each other's welfare, and lifted their spirits when times were hard. They signed their letters, "Thine in the bonds of womanhood," "Thine in the bonds of fellowship for the oppressed," "Thy sister in Jesus," and "In the best of bonds." The power *among* these women was so extraordinary it led one scholar, Julie Roy Jeffrey, to observe that the "antislavery community drew its strength from shared feelings and a sense of personal intimacy between women." You can't be interconnected in the patriarchy because it is organized from the top down. Still, even a horizontal relationship needs a technology of relationality to remain connected. This new relational process has, at its core, structured conversation, where people take turns talking, to ensure safety. When a person doesn't trust they'll be understood, anxiety forms and one's energy goes straight to the lower brain, known as the reptilian brain, which triggers cortisol, the chemical that tells us "fight or flight." It's a black and white reaction of either shutting down or becoming defensive (or offensive). But when people learn how to talk in a way that is safer—meaning both parties have a chance to speak and the listener sounds back what she is hearing again and again, until she gets it right—their energy can get to the upper brain, firing the cerebral cortex, where they can create collaboration. Thus, learning to talk to and value one another is one of the most radical activist actions you can take.

TWO: Include your faith voice in your political voice.

A faith practice is useful to help us get beyond triggering and reacting, and reaching beyond that first reaction to empathy. Having a mantra or a Psalm to call on is part of the practice of lower-brain, reactive thinking. In order for me to even remember the Twenty-Third Psalm, I have to go into the upper brain, and that takes me out of anxiety. This is in part why I believe that spiritual practice and a mantra of choice contributes to the development of a healthy brain. You are not going to create a healthy world if you stay in the lower "my way or the highway" brain.

In 1995 I, along with thirty thousand others, attended the United Nations Fourth World Conference on Women and the Environment, held in Beijing. For some time I had been quietly struggling with a sense of dissonance in my own experience as a feminist who was also a woman of faith. I was driven to learn whether there were distinct dynamics fueling activism based on whether a woman identified as faith-based or secular. Were there differences in methodology as well as perspective? And if so, might the two groups create a sense of unity?

In Beijing I conducted a study, looking for answers. The response was overwhelming— thoughtful, complex, passionate, and, in its own way, beautiful—and troubling. The study definitively showed there was a deep rift. The two groups did not trust the other's motivations or practices. "The more rigid women's groups are in their religious beliefs or in their commitment to a secular perspective," feminist writer Letty Cottin Pogrebin once told me, "the more likely they are to be in conflict and incapable of engaging in coalition."

My response to this reality check was to devote myself to a larger question: How do we embrace the broad range of differences in our midst, be they religious, ethnic, gender, or socioeconomic? This is *our* holy cause. And it is urgent, because we have much work to do.

We can begin by acknowledging that those who work for social justice, the environment, and peace are engaged in a spiritual way of being. In *The Redemption of God*, the feminist theologian Carter Heyward blends together faith and relationality in this observation: "We are never called forth alone but always to answer the Spirit's call *with* one another. . . . [A]t the core of our faith, we know that in the beginning and in the end, we are not alone. In our living and in our dying, we are not separate from one another."

What if the values being preached from the pulpit reflected this spirit of empathy, love, and caring that brings people together rather than driving them apart? What if our definition of faith was expanded beyond narrow creeds to the full recognition of the human drive for greater consciousness and compassion? I feel deeply connected to the words, example, and living spirit of Christ, and I don't need a church or religious leader to mediate that relationship. I know God.

I am just as critical of the hypocrisy and oppression undertaken in the name of God, but I feel we must acknowledge the chasm that exists today between secular feminists and feminists of faith and face it honestly and not dismiss it as a forbidden topic.

In the end, the most important thing to remember is that faith itself, across religions, is a call to love and care for one another. Christians are *mandated* to love one another. A major theme of the Gospels is God's love for us and how we are to love others, and that the fruit of our faith will be that love. "Teacher, which is the greatest commandment?" Jesus was asked. He replied, "Love the Lord your God with all your heart and with all your soul and with all your mind. This is the first and greatest commandment. And the second is like it: Love your neighbor as yourself." What better message can there be than this—and what better argument for the secular and religious to unite in feminism?

THREE: Heal the dissociation, externally and interiorly

The United States remains ensnared in the reverberations of our early sins against women and people of color, but profoundly and distinctly against women of color. We are often encouraged to see women's rights and racial justice as on parallel or even competing tracks. Just as abolition and women's rights, in some ways, became weaker when treated as distinct and placed in competition with one another. This dissociation in our midst can be healed with actions that promote inclusion.

The abolitionist women would counsel us to unite disparate movements under the overarching truth that all human life is sacred and the rights of all individuals should be protected. Their methodology was truly democratic and lateral; it was interracial and inclusive of men and women. They weren't single-issue activists but looked at the whole, and although the language wasn't coined, their understanding of their cause was intersectional. We must embrace all with a "both/and" rubric of inclusion—one that brings into the fold those who have traditionally been excluded by mainstream feminism—among them women of color, men, mothers, and people of faith. Following the blueprint of the early feminist abolitionists will help us shift our values from either/or to both/and. We will then be able to work collaboratively to resolve our different philosophies and opinions, and work together to cocreate a shared global social justice movement.

The dissociation in our communities exists in the hearts of women as well. I was grateful to continue to recover our radical women's history, but it was the suppression of the religious or spiritual piece of the story of feminism that lingered in my consciousness. I've struggled to make sense of *why* the Christian part of these feminists' lives would be edited out of their stories. I've come to the conclusion that the rejection was not because women are more powerful when unencumbered by faith, but because segregating any part of themselves means that they become *less* powerful. Women, including feminist women, often disassociate from power, perhaps in part because they've experienced damage from people having power over them. We know we are powerful, but we don't trust what we know—what Carol Gilligan calls "the split within." We are looking for a different way to express ourselves, and it resonates deeply with me that feminists both critique power and identify with vulnerability. It's violent not to have statues of women in Central Park and to leave women out of history books. The result of all of this violence is why, when women are given a chance to step into power, they often can't. Our first step toward doing so might be to acknowledge our sacred spirit.

FOUR: Partner with men

Gloria Steinem's observation that "a feminist is anyone who recognizes the equality and full humanity of women and men" strikes me as an important statement about our need to partner with men in achieving our goals. The abolitionist women had strong male partners, such as William Lloyd Garrison, whose support for their cause and their right to speak out enabled them to thrive against phenomenal social pressure. Today we know that the battle for gender equality involves all of us, women and men working in concert, yet much of the language of women's rights comes from a place of oppression, so men are often made to feel that they are being blamed. An emphasis on relationality leads us to acknowledge that power comes from working together, not shaming the other. Our target should be the larger conflict within the culture where men, too, are victims of social pressure and unrealistic expectations. We can heal the gender wounds by practicing empathy for one another, striving to understand the "other" and welcome him or her into our circle.

On a practical level, we need both women and men to do the work of feminism. Women alone cannot end the scourges of sexual harassment, nor can we reach full empowerment in the halls of government or the corporate world without aligning ourselves with men who support these goals. How can we make this happen? First, we can raise our sons to have a natural tendency toward inclusiveness. In our adult relationships, we can resist the impulse to stay silent when the men in our lives speak or act without respect, and help them understand their error without attacking them. And I can attest that I have no greater friends than my husband and my brother Ray. Whenever I need help in my work with women, I know I can turn to both of them.

FIVE: Be hungry for history—and recover it.

How could history have forgotten these women? They should be household names, like Eleanor Roosevelt and Rosa Parks, yet we never hear of them. There are no memorials on any American plaza to inform the generations of a time when women lived such courage. Many were literally willing to die for the justice they sought. Their stories are emerging at a time when we have a great need to draw on their example.

These abolitionist feminists stepped into power but were deliberately left out of history. When I learned about these foremothers, I was incredulous and grew truly furious. I began to feel it was my sacred duty to do right by these women—to learn from them personally and enable the larger culture to learn about and from them. Now you, reader, have had a chance to take in their correspondence and their bravery in identifying and confronting the outrageous, inhumane injustices that were normalized in their time. We honor them by letting their spirit animate our own lives and bringing a consciousness of the bold sacred activism on behalf of justice.

SIX: Don't agonize—*organize*.

One hundred and eighty years ago, Angelina Grimké said that the work of the abolitionist women would "turn the world upside down." She and her sisters believed that all things were possible. Yet the backlash was so fierce, and the patriarchy so strong, that the world-changing effort they began has been a constant struggle—one often ridiculed and submerged. In time, struggle can wear away the will. Even with important advances the feminist movement of today swims against new tides. In our exhaustion we often settle for small victories, although now global needs are urgent and call for a big vision. Although we possess civil rights and a public voice the abolitionist sisterhood could have only dreamed of, we need to do something bold with our privilege. We have the relational tools to do just that and by thinking big we can complete the human agenda for freedom and equality. We, too, can be possessed by that rare spirit that moves civilization forward.

But it's not enough to think big; we must *do* something with our power. We must step up, step out, and act. Perform a spirited practice of social activism, and do it every day. Don't just read about the state of the world, complain, and wring your hands. Make the decision to move something forward. Find a community that wants to make change happen, and be a part of that community. Even small acts have a ripple effect: join an organization, write a letter, volunteer once a week, send a check once a month, sign a petition, march, join a protest. Become engaged in making change happen. The January 21, 2017, Women's March on Washington began as a single demoralized post on Facebook and became a phenomenon that included almost seven hundred sister marches around the world. The Women's March was a powerful organic expression of relational power—the belief that by organizing together change is possible. Spiritually more than just a one-day event, it had all the signposts of the way great movements begin. The March demonstrated that, like the abolitionist women, we have the power to turn our own world upside down. More than knowing our own strength, we have to use it. It will do your soul good.

SEVEN: Promote a feminist agape.

We need to promote agape—a very radical love—within the women's movement today, to create a wave of feminism that is truly inclusive. We need a feminism that upholds what is at the heart of every human rights effort and what the women's movement is uniquely poised to help promote: equality for all. Equality, mutuality, is the path to a social love. This is the ideal held up by the early feminist abolitionists. Their work was motivated by love—a love rooted in their faith and born from empathy. Nothing on earth is more powerful than that force. And we now have the tools available to defeat the paradigms of isolation, competition, and domination, through a living, breathing action-based ethic of love.

Abolition was a movement to restore connection in a culture ruptured and split apart by a racial divide. This rupture catalyzed a response—a sympathetic (empathic) feeling from the population. It was a view in which even some privileged citizens felt themselves connected to and took responsibility for the suffering of the disenfranchised. *Agape* is the Greek word meaning "God's love," but it is the capacity to love someone heedlessly and unconditionally. "'This is a cause worth dying for" are the words of agape. These women were willing to sacrifice themselves. What courage! The most significant social change are movements built around the spirit and ethic of love.

The abolitionists were visionaries, both women and men who called for congruence between the democratic ethic and its practice. They were faith-based activists who called for a seamless integration between the teachings of Christ and the dogma of church doctrine. They were active during a time when the culture was in denial about its false morality and double standard. The government espoused "freedom and justice for all," while at the same time creating and protecting laws that lifted up slavery. The country had dissociated the creed it espoused from the laws and the life of its citizens. The Christian faith that preached the sanctity of all life had become institutionalized in forms that fractured the unity of love. Many Christian churches either condoned slavery or looked the other way. It was only as more people tapped into the power of a personal faith and the vision of Christian unity that a new ethic of empathy began healing the soul of the nation.

Now, when our culture is fracturing in ever-greater ways, it is even more urgent to once again lift up and wield love. As Dr. Cornel West has said, "Never forget that justice is what love looks like in public. . . . We have to be militants for kindness, subversive for sweetness, and radicals for tenderness." Love is the impulse that exists between parent and child; the force that drives both secular and faith-based activists; and the foundation upon which healthy partnerships can be built. Love beats at the heart of feminism. As we use the blueprint of the early abolitionist feminists to construct a new and stronger feminism, love is the most urgent and necessary tool available to us.

WHEN I DISCOVERED the abolitionist women I was overwhelmed. I could think of nothing else. As I felt their spirit fill me, I wanted to bring that inspiration into my own work and tell the world about this time in our history when women acted with such courage and conviction, against all odds.

I feel somewhat akin to these women. I have wanted to articulate the ways I see the energies of faith and feminism united in the world today; I wanted to tell the truth about how I, surrounded by wealth, would never have dared to own my power had I not felt the strength of God in me—something larger than my brothers, father, culture, and upbringing. When I held the letters and read the words of Lucretia, Angelina, Sarah, Grace, and the others, I finally had the historical documentation that supported my conviction that faith and feminism have experienced a synergistic relationship for a long time.

Faith. Relationship. Empathy. These are the three legs of courage that support brave acts, large and small, in our own lives and on behalf of others. It is only now, at this moment in time, that a full realization of this energy is even possible. Every year new imperatives emerge in the culture, reaching into our lives to locate our missing pieces and release the silent parts of ourselves. How wonderful that we have these women as faithful companions from another era to take our hands as we continue, boldly and joyfully, along this path.

I am grateful to be a feminist and to add my labor to such meaningful work. I'm conscious that I stand on the shoulders of those who came before me. Would I have a voice today were it not for early feminists who demanded theirs be heard? Would I have such a strong sense of the congruence of Christianity and feminism had they not drawn so explicitly on their own faith to fuel their mission? In everything I do, these women guide me. And I see their legacy in so much of what is working well within human rights movements worldwide, although the organizers of these movements don't necessarily realize this.

The women whose stories are told in this book crafted a radical blueprint for movement building and widened a pathway for the women's struggles today. Our current social and political climate echoes the era in which the early abolitionist feminists organized. The dissociative split between the ideals our country espouses and the way whole populations are marginalized and demeaned (even killed) continues, to tragic ends for all of us. While a multitude of human rights movements speak out against this dissonance, the focus on issue-based advocacy often splinters us. The early abolitionist women taught us the power of interracial organizing, feminist values, and the fearlessness that can accompany knowing the Creator and the belief in our fundamental equality in God's eyes. Their lives are a testament to a courage that is grounded in faith, strengthened in relationships, and inspired by empathy for the marginalized.

These women were written out of mainstream feminist history. Yet their message lives on. They wanted to be free to engage intellect and honor their belief in self. Their understanding that we are of equal value and all children of God remains a radical and powerful vision. I feel honored to help usher these women out of the shadows of history. I hope they have become as alive to you as they are to me. Their lives are a potent reminder of the great healing that can occur when women emerge from their exile and attempt to reconcile our often wretched nation with its amazing ideals.

NOTES

INTRODUCTION

1. Sarah Louisa Forten, "An Appeal to Women," in *She Wields a Pen: American Women Poets of the Nineteenth Century*, ed. Janet Gray (Iowa City, IA: University of Iowa Press, 1997).

2. Wednesday Martin, *Primates of Park Avenue: A Memoir* (New York: Simon & Schuster, 2015).

3. Susan Savion, *Quoting Matilda* (Bloomington, IN: Author House, 2015).

CHAPTER ONE: Band of Sisters

1. Louis Filler, *The Crusade against Slavery 1830–1860* (Piscataway, NJ: Transaction Publishers, 2011).

2. Lee V. Chambers, *The Weston Sisters: An American Abolitionist Family* (Chapel Hill, NC: University of North Carolina Press, 2015).

3. Barbara Welter, "The Cult of True Womanhood: 1820–1860," *American Quarterly* 18, no. 2 (Summer 1966): 151–74.

4. Henry Mayer, *All On Fire: Lloyd Garrison and the Abolition of Slavery* (New York: W. W. Norton, 1998).

5. Richard S. Newman, *The Transformation of American Abolitionism: Fighting Slavery in the Early Republic* (Chapel Hill, NC: University of North Carolina Press, 2002).

6. Boston Female Anti-Slavery Society, *Right and Wrong in Boston* (Boston: Anti-Slavery Society, 1836).

7. John Gatta, *American Madonna: Images of Divine Women*

in Literary Culture (New York: Oxford University Press, 1997). Fuller, a leading intellectual of the nineteenth century, is known for her literary criticism, journalism, and her writing of the first feminist manifesto in the United States. She was influenced by the Marian ideal, *mater gloriosa*, and felt that beyond equality, women needed to strive for divinity.

8. Peter P. Hinks, *To Awaken My Afflicted Brethren: David Walker and the Problem of Antebellum Slave Resistance* (University Park, PA: Pennsylvania State University Press, 1997).

9. Benjamin Quarles, *Black Abolitionists* (New York: DaCapo Press, 1991).

10. Maria W. Stewart, "Religion and the Pure Principles of Morality, the Sure Foundation on Which We Must Build," in *Maria W. Stewart: America's First Black Woman Political Writer,* ed. Marilyn Richardson (Bloomington, IN: Indiana University Press, 1987), 28–42; Maria W. Stewart, "An Address at the African Masonic Hall," in *Ripples of Hope: Great American Civil Rights Speeches*, ed. Josh Gottheimer (New York: Basic Civitas, 2004), 14–18.

11. Margaret Hope Bacon, *Valiant Friend: The Life of Lucretia Mott* (Philadelphia: Friends General Conference, 1999).

12. Brian Dorsey, *Reforming Men and Women: Gender in the Antebellum City* (Ithaca, NY: Cornell University Press, 2006); Aileen Kraditor, *Means and Ends in American Abolitionism: Garrison and His Critics on Strategy and Tactics 1834–1850* (Lanham, MD: Ivan R. Dee, 1989).

13. Samuel J. May, *Some Recollections of Our Antislavery Conflict* (Boston: Fields, Osgood & Co., 1869).

14. Otelia Cromwell, *Lucretia Mott* (Cambridge, MA: Harvard University Press, 1958).

15. Ruth Bogin and Jean Fagan Yellin, "Introduction," in *The Abolitionist Sisterhood: Women's Political Culture in Antebellum America*, eds. Jean Fagan Yellin and John C. Van Horne

(Ithaca, NY: Cornell University Press, 1994). There were four black delegates out of seventy-one, making the black presence 6 percent of delegates; and fourteen black corresponding members out of 104, making the ratio of corresponding members about 14 percent black.

16. Phillis Wheatley, *Poems on Various Subjects, Religious and Moral* (London: A. Bell, 1773).

17. Elizabeth B. Clark, "'The Sacred Rights of the Weak': Pain, Sympathy, and the Culture of Individual Rights in Antebellum America," *Journal of American History* 82, no. 2 (September 1995): 463–93. Abolitionist white women explained that prayer gave them sympathy for the slave. They claimed that the study of scripture and religious texts revealed a God-ordained responsibility to advocate for those in slavery.

18. Chambers, *The Weston Sisters*.

19. Chapman [on behalf of BFASS] to Mary Grew [PFASS], 12 January 1837, Historical Society of Pennsylvania, quoted in Phillip Lapsansky (curator), *"We Abolition Women Are Turning the World Upside Down!": An Exhibition Commemorating the 150th Anniversary of the Anti-Slavery Conventions of American Women, 1837, 1838, 1839* (booklet accompanying exhibit, Philadelphia: Library Company of Philadelphia, 1989).

CHAPTER TWO: A Convention Like No Other

1. Dorothy Sterling, *Turning the World Upside Down: The Anti-Slavery Convention of American Women Held in New York City May 9–12, 1837* (New York: Feminist Press, 1987).

2. Louis Ruchames, ed., *The Letters of William Lloyd Garrison, Volume II: A House Dividing Against Itself, 1836–1840* (Cambridge, MA: Belknap Press, 1971).

3. Amy Swerdlow, "The Ladies' New York Anti-Slavery Societies" in *The Abolitionist Sisterhood: Women's Political Culture*

in Antebellum America, eds. Jean Fagan Yellin and John C. Van Horne (Ithaca, NY: Cornell University Press, 1994).

4. Larry Ceplair, ed., *The Public Years of Sarah and Angelina Grimké, Selected Writings 1835–1839* (New York: Columbia University Press, 1989).

5. Quoted in Phillip Lapsansky (curator), "*We Abolition Women Are Turning the World Upside Down!": An Exhibition Commemorating the 150th Anniversary of the Anti-Slavery Conventions of American Women, 1837, 1838, 1839* (booklet accompanying exhibit. Philadelphia: Library Company of Philadelphia, 1989).

6. Gerda Lerner, *The Grimké Sisters from South Carolina: Pioneers for Women's Rights and Abolition* (Chapel Hill, NC: University of North Carolina Press, 2004).

7. Sarah Grimké, "Education of Women," box 21, Weld-Grimké Family Papers, William L. Clements Library (Ann Arbor, MI: The University of Michigan).

8. Theodore Dwight Weld, et al., *Angelina Grimké Weld: Born in Charleston, South Carolina, February 20, 1805; Died in Hyde Park, Massachusetts, October 26, 1879* (Boston: George H. Ellis, 1880), 19.

9. Angelina Grimké, diary entry, 1828, quoted in Stephen Howard Browne, *Angelina Grimké: Rhetoric, Identity, and the Radical Imagination* (East Lansing, MI: Michigan State University Press, 1999), 35.

10. Katherine DuPre Lumpkin, *The Emancipation of Angelina Grimké* (Chapel Hill, NC: University of North Carolina Press, 1974).

11. A. Grimké to S. Grimké, 3 July 1836, Theodore Dwight Weld Papers (Washington, DC: Library of Congress), quoted in Gilbert Hobbs Barnes, *The Anti-Slavery Impulse 1830–1844* (Gloucester, MA: Peter Smith Publisher Inc., 1964), 154.

12. Catherine H. Birney, *The Grimké Sisters: Sarah and An-*

gelina Grimké, the First American Advocates of Abolition and Women's Rights (Boston: Lee and Shepard, 1885).

13. Angelina Emily Grimké, An Appeal to the Christian Women of the South, (New York: American Anti-Slavery Society, 1836).

14. Elizabeth McHenry, Forgotten Readers: Recovering the Lost History of African American Literary Societies (Durham, NC: Duke University Press, 2002).

15. S. Douglass to William Basset, December 1837, Weld-Grimké Collection, William L. Clements Library (Ann Arbor, MI: University of Michigan), quoted in Charles Johnson et al., Africans in America (New York: Harcourt, Brace & Co., 1999).

16. Julie Roy Jeffrey, The Great Silent Army of Abolitionism: Ordinary Women in the Antislavery Movement (Chapel Hill, NC: University of North Carolina Press, 1998).

17. S. Douglass to William Basset, December 1837, Weld-Grimké Collection, William L. Clements Library (Ann Arbor, MI: University of Michigan).

18. Sarah Louisa Forten, "An Appeal to Woman," in She Wields a Pen: American Women Poets of the Nineteenth Century, ed. Janet Gray (Iowa City, IA: University of Iowa Press, 1997).

19. Sterling, Turning the World Upside Down.

20. Ibid.

21. Ibid.

22. Ibid.

CHAPTER THREE: A Public Voice

1. At the close of Angelina Grimké's speech at Pennsylvania Hall in 1838, she attributed this quote to the British Parliament with the hopes that US legislators would act similarly.

2. Constance L. Jackson, *Over the River . . . Life of Lydia Maria Child, Abolitionist for Freedom, 1802–1880: Companion Book to the Epic Documentary* (Rolling Hills Estates, CA: Permanent Productions, 2008).

3. Dorothy Sterling, *Turning the World Upside Down: The Anti-Slavery Convention of American Women, Held in New York City May 9–12, 1837* (New York: Feminist Press, 1987).

4. Ibid.

5. Ibid.

6. Ibid.

7. Ibid.

8. Ibid.

9. Van Broekhoven and Deborah Bingham, "'Let Your Names Be Enrolled': Method and Ideology in Women's Antislavery Petitioning," in *The Abolitionist Sisterhood*, eds. Jean Fagan Yellin and John C. Van Horne (Ithaca, NY: Cornell University Press, 1994), 179–99.

10. Gerda Lerner, *The Grimké Sisters from South Carolina: Pioneers for Women's Rights and Abolition* (Chapel Hill: University of North Carolina Press, 1967).

11. Theodore Dwight Weld, *In Memory: Angelina Grimké Weld* (Boston: George Ellis, 1880).

12. Sterling, *Turning the World*.

13. Van Broekhoven and Bingham, "'Let Your Names Be Enrolled,'" 182.

14. Ibid.

15. S. Grimké to Jane Smith, 24 January 1839, Grimké-Weld Papers, William L. Clements Library (Ann Arbor, MI: University of Michigan), quoted in Gerda Lerner, *The Grimké Sisters from South Carolina* (Chapel Hill, NC: University of North Carolina Press), 205.

16. Julie Roy Jeffrey, *The Great Silent Army of Abolitionism: Ordinary Women in the Antislavery Movement* (Chapel Hill, NC: University of North Carolina Press, 1998).

17. Gilbert Hobbs Barnes, *The Anti-Slavery Impulse: 1830–1844* (Gloucester, MA: Peter Smith Publisher Inc., 1964).

18. Larry Ceplair, ed., *The Public Years of Sarah and Angelina Grimké, Selected Writings 1835–1839* (New York: Columbia University Press, 1989).

19. Catherine H. Birney, *The Grimké Sisters: Sarah and Angelina Grimké, the First American Advocates of Abolition and Women's Rights* (Boston: Lee and Shepard, 1885).

20. Gilbert H. Barnes and Dwight L. Dumond, eds., *The Letters of Theodore Dwight Weld, Angelina Grimké Weld and Sarah Grimké 1822–1844* (Gloucester, MA: Peter Smith Publishers, 1965).

21. Ibid.

22. Ibid.

23. Norma Basch, "Invisible Women: The Legal Fiction of Marital Unity in Nineteenth-Century America," *Feminist Studies* 5, no. 2 (1979).

24. Larry Ceplair, ed., *The Public Years*.

25. Gerda Lerner, *The Grimké Sisters from South Carolina: Pioneers for Women's Rights and Abolition* (Chapel Hill: University of North Carolina Press, 1967).

CHAPTER FOUR: *Fiery Backlash*

1. The following resolutions are from *Proceedings of the Anti-Slavery Convention of American Women Held in Philadelphia, May 15, 16, 17, 18, 1838* (Philadelphia: Merrihew and Gunn, 1838).

2. Archibald Henry Grimké, *William Lloyd Garrison: The Abolitionist* (New York: Funk & Wagnalls, 1891).

3. Samuel Webb, *History of Pennsylvania Hall Which Was Destroyed by a Mob on the 17th of May, 1838* (Philadelphia: Merrihew and Gunn, 1838). This was Angelina Grimké's last public speech and the only one that was transcribed.

4. Wendell Phillips Garrison and Francis Jackson Garrison, *William Lloyd Garrison, 1805–1879: The Story of His Life Told by His Children, Volume 3* (New York: The Century Co., 1885).

5. Webb, *History of Pennsylvania Hall*.

6. Ibid.

7. Bartholomew Fussell to Edwin, 23 May 1838, Lewis-Fussell Family Papers, RG5/087, Friends Historical Library of Swarthmore College.

8. Quoted in Phillip Lapsansky (curator), *"We Abolition Women Are Turning the World Upside Down!": An Exhibition Commemorating the 150th Anniversary of the Anti-Slavery Conventions of American Women, 1837, 1838, 1839* (booklet accompanying exhibit. Philadelphia: Library Company of Philadelphia, 1989).

CHAPTER FIVE: *Walking with God*

1. Angelina Grimké, *An Appeal to the Christian Women of the South* (New York: American Anti-Slavery Society, 1836).

2. Ibid.

3. Angelina Grimké, *Letters to Catherine E. Beecher, in Reply to an Essay on Slavery and Abolitionism, Addressed to A. E. Grimké, Revised by the Author* (Boston: Isaac Knapp, 1838).

4. Miriam Schneir, ed. *Feminism: The Essential Historical Writings* (New York: Random House, 1972).

5. Sarah Moore Grimké, *An Epistle to the Clergy of the Southern States* (New York, 1836).

6. Hubbard Winslow, *"The Appropriate Sphere of Woman": A Discourse Delivered in the Bowdoin Street Church, July 9, 1837* (Boston: Weeks, Jordan and Co., 1837).

7. James Brewer Stewart, *Holy Warriors: The Abolitionists and American Slavery* (New York: Hill and Wang, 1976).

8. Marie J. Lindhorst, *Sarah Mapps Douglass: The Emer-*

gence of an African American Educator/Activist in Nineteenth Century Philadelphia (PhD diss., Pennsylvania State University, 1995).

9. Samuel Webb, *History of Pennsylvania Hall Which Was Destroyed by a Mob on the 17th of May, 1838* (Philadelphia: Merrihew and Gunn, 1838).

10. Angelina Grimké, diary entry, 1828, quoted in Stephen Howard Browne, *Angelina Grimké: Rhetoric, Identity, and the Radical Imagination* (East Lansing, MI: Michigan State University Press, 1999).

11. Sue Morgan and Jacqueline deVries, eds., *Women, Gender and Religious Cultures in Britain, 1800–1940* (New York: Routledge, 2010).

CHAPTER SIX: Sympathy for the Woman

1. A. Grimké Weld to Anna Frost, 18 August 1839, Grimké-Weld Papers, (Washington, DC: Library of Congress), quoted in Gerda Lerner, *The Grimké Sisters from South Carolina: Pioneers for Women's Rights and Abolition* (Chapel Hill, NC: University of North Carolina Press, 1967).

2. A. Kelley to Theodore Weld, 14 January 1839, Weld-Grimké Letters, vol. 2, quoted in Dorothy Sterling, *Ahead of Her Time: Abby Kelley and the Politics of Antislavery* (New York: W. W. Norton & Co., 1991).

3. Gilbert H. Barnes and Dwight L. Dumond, eds., *The Letters of Theodore Dwight Weld, Angelina Grimké Weld and Sarah Grimké 1822–1844* (Gloucester, MA: Peter Smith Publishers, 1965).

4. Anna Davis Hallowell, ed., *James and Lucretia Mott: Life and Letters* (Boston: Houghton, Mifflin and Co., 1890).

5. Beverly Wilson Palmer, ed., *Selected Letters of Lucretia Coffin Mott* (Champaign, IL: University of Illinois Press, 2002).

6. *Proceedings of the Anti-Slavery Convention of American Women Held in Philadelphia, May 1st, 2nd and 3rd, 1839* (Philadelphia: Merrihew and Thompson, 1839).

7. Manisha Sinha, *The Slave's Cause: A History of Abolition* (New Haven, CT: Yale University Press, 2016).

8. Margaret Hope Bacon, *I Speak for My Slave Sister: The Life of Abby Kelley Foster* (New York: Thomas Cromwell Co., 1974).

9. Dorothy Sterling, *Ahead of Her Time: Abby Kelley and the Politics of Antislavery* (New York: W. W. Norton, 1994).

10. Phebe A. Hanaford, *Daughters of America, or Women of the Century* (Augusta, ME: True and Company, 1883).

11. Belle Squire, *The Woman Movement in America: A Short Account of the Struggle for Equal Rights* (Chicago: A.C. McClurg and Co., 1911).

12. Lucretia Mott, *Slavery and "The Woman Question": Lucretia Mott's Diary of Her Visit to Great Britain to Attend the World's Anti-Slavery Convention of 1840*, ed. Frederick B. Tolles (Haverford, PA: Friends Historical Society, 1952).

13. Ira V. Brown, *Mary Grew: Abolitionist and Feminist, 1813–1896* (Selinsgrove, PA: Susquehanna University Press, 1991).

14. Elizabeth Cady Stanton, *Eighty Years and More: Reminiscences 1815–1897* (New York: T. Fisher Unwin, 1898).

15. Jean Fagan Yellin and John C. Van Horne, *The Abolitionist Sisterhood: Women's Political Culture in Antebellum America* (Ithaca, NY: Cornell University Press, 1994).

16. Judith Wellman, *The Road to Seneca Falls: Elizabeth Cady Stanton and the First Woman's Rights Convention* (Champaign, IL: University of Illinois Press, 2004).

17. Lori D. Ginzberg, *Elizabeth Cady Stanton: An American Life* (New York: Hill and Wang, 2009).

CHAPTER SEVEN: A Bodyguard of Hearts

1. A. Grimké to S. Douglass, 25 February 1838, Grimké-Weld Papers, William L. Clements Library (Ann Arbor, MI: University of Michigan), quoted in Anna M. Speicher, *Religious World of Antislavery Women* (Syracuse, NY: Syracuse University Press, 2000).

2. "Reminiscences of Abby Kelley Foster by Her Daughter Alla W. Foster on the Fortieth Anniversary of the First National Women's Rights Convention," *The Women's Journal* 12, no. 6 (February 7, 1891).

3. Dorothy Sterling, *Ahead of Her Time: Abby Kelley and the Politics of Antislavery* (New York: W. W. Norton, 1994).

4. Ibid.

5. Phebe A. Hanaford, *Daughters of America or Women of the Century* (Augusta, ME: True & Co., 1883).

6. Dorothy Sterling, *Ahead of Her Time.*

7. Abby Kelley Foster Papers 1837–1887, Haverford College Libraries (Haverford, PA); Lydia Maria Child Papers, William L. Clements Library (Ann Arbor, MI: University of Michigan).

8. Jean Fagan Yellin, *Women and Sisters: The Antislavery Feminists in American Culture* (New Haven, CT: Yale University Press, 1989).

9. S. Douglass to Josiah White, Josiah White Papers, 1876. Quaker Collection. Haverford College Libraries (Haverford, PA).

10. Ibid.

11. Gilbert H. Barnes and Dwight L. Dumond, eds. *The Letters of Theodore Dwight Weld, Angelina Grimké Weld and Sarah Grimké 1822–1844* (Gloucester, MA: Peter Smith Publisher Inc., 1965).

12. "A Tribute of Respect to the Veteran Teacher," 1898, Slaughter College, Trevor Arnett Library, Atlanta University

Center Library, quoted in Shirley J. Yee, *Black Women Abolitionists* (Knoxville, TN: University of Tennessee Press, 1992).

13. *View of the Subject of Slavery Contained in the Biblical Repertory for April 1836* (Pittsburg, PA: 1836).

14. Ira V. Brown, *Mary Grew: Abolitionist and Feminist, 1813–1896* (Selinsgrove, PA: Susquehanna University Press, 1991).

15. *Proceedings of the Woman's Rights Convention Held at Westchester, PA, June 2nd and 3rd, 1852* (Philadelphia, PA: Merrihew and Thompson, 1852).

16. Ira V. Brown, *Mary Grew*.

17. John Greenleaf Whittier, *The Writings of John Greenleaf Whittier in Seven Volumes, Volume 4* (London: MacMillan and Co, 1889).

18. Ira V. Brown, *Mary Grew*.

19. Elizabeth Cady Stanton, *Eighty Years and More: Reminiscences 1815–1897* (New York: T. Fisher Unwin, 1898); Lori D. Ginzberg, *Elizabeth Cady Stanton: An American Life* (New York: Hill and Wang, 2010).

20. Anna Howard Shaw, "Eulogy Delivered at Susan B. Anthony's Funeral," Papers of Elizabeth Cady Stanton and Susan B. Anthony, Rutgers University, http://www.ecssba.rutgers.edu/docs/shaw.html.

21. Larry G. Murphy, *Sojourner Truth: A Biography* (Santa Barbara, CA: Greenwood, 2001).

22. Yet when Phyllis Schlafly died in 2016, at the age of ninety-two, her biography showed her to be far from the "traditional" woman she promoted. A run for Congress, a law degree in her fifties, and a lifetime of organizing and activism belied her central tenet that women belonged in traditional roles. It's interesting to note that on her wedding day in 1949 she removed the word "obey" from her vows.

23. Gloria Steinem, "Testimony before Senate Hearings on the Equal Rights Amendment," May 6, 1970.

APPENDIX A

Timeline of the Abolitionist Women's Movement

1780
- Pennsylvania legislature passes An Act for the Gradual Abolition of Slavery, which was one of the first US attempts at curtailing slavery.

1782
- Grace Douglass (neé Bustill) is born in Burlington, New Jersey, to Cyrus Bustill, a freedman, and Elizabeth Morrey, the daughter of an Englishman and a Native American woman.

1802
- Lydia Maria Child (neé Francis) is born in Medford, Massachusetts.

1805
- Angelina Emily Grimké is born in Charleston, South Carolina. Her sister Sarah becomes her godmother.

1808
- Congress bans the transatlantic slave trade.

1817

- Thomas Coffin Mott, Lucretia's first-born son, dies at age two. The death of her "beloved Tommy" sobers her and starts her on her journey toward the ministry.

1819

- Aware of racism in the white schools, Grace Douglass and James Forten found a school for black children in Philadelphia. Sarah Douglass, a student at this school, would later teach there.

1821

- Unhappy with the slave system in her native South Carolina, Sarah Moore Grimké moves to Philadelphia.
- Lucretia Mott is officially recognized as a minister in the Quaker community.

1824

- Child publishes *Hobomok* at age twenty-two; it becomes a best seller.

1826

- Child publishes the first issue of the *Juvenile Miscellany*, a popular magazine for children.

1827

- There is a split in the Society of Friends. Lucretia and James Mott decide to follow one of the founders of Nine Partners School, the fiery Elias Hicks, and join the Hicksite sect.

1828

- Lydia Maria Child marries David Lee Child.

1829

- Lydia Maria Child publishes the internationally successful *American Frugal Housewife*.
- Sarah Grimké convinces her sister Angelina to join her in Philadelphia, and they become "voluntary exiles from the blood-stained soil of South Carolina."

1831

- In January William Lloyd Garrison publishes the first issue of the *Liberator*, the Boston-based abolitionist newspaper
- Child meets Garrison and says that he "got hold of the strings of my conscience and pulled me into reforms. . . . Old dreams vanished, old associates departed and all things became new."
- Sarah Douglass joins several other women to form the Female Literary Association (FLA) of Philadelphia.
- Nat Turner's Rebellion, a bloody slave revolt, causes many towns, including Philadelphia, to enact restrictive laws against blacks.

1832

- The FLA invites Garrison to one of their meetings. He reports, "[I]f the traducers of the Negro race could be acquainted with the moral worth, just refinement, and large intelligence of this association, their mouths would be hereafter dumb." He welcomes pieces for the *Liberator* written by FLA members.
- In February the Anti-Slavery Society (Salem, Massachusetts) is founded by black women.
- In July Rhode Island women establish an antislavery society.

1833

- Child publishes *An Appeal in Favor of that Class of Americans Called Africans*, a significant antislavery tract.
- Sarah Douglass writes to poet and abolitionist Elizabeth Chandler to express her appreciation for the work that the abolitionists are doing. She is also invited to New York to teach at a Free African School for Girls. She stays a year.
- In December Mott founds the Philadelphia Female Anti-Slavery Society (PFASS) after being banned from signing the constitution of the American Anti-Slavery Society (AAS). Grace Douglass is one of the founding members.
- The *North American Review* ranks Child as America's most notable woman writer.
- The British Emancipation Act is promulgated, ending slavery in the West Indies; female abolitionists are credited with much of its success.

1834

- The first antislavery fair, led by Child and Maria Weston Chapman, is held at the Anti-Slavery Office in Boston.
- An anti-abolition mob destroys forty homes in Philadelphia's black community.
- The Colored Female Anti-Slavery Society (CFASS) is founded in Middletown, Connecticut.
- The Chatham Street Chapel Society, the first women's New York City abolitionist group, is founded.

1835

- Pro-slavery mobs bully abolitionists in cities throughout the North, causing William Lloyd Garrison to dub it a "reign of terror."
- Angelina Grimké joins PFASS and writes a letter to Garri-

son, which, when published in the *Liberator*, will bring her to the forefront of the antislavery crusade.

- The Ladies' New York City Anti-Slavery Society (LNYCASS) is formed, and the women join the antislavery petitioning campaign.
- Oberlin College begins to accept black male students.

1836

- The Pinckney Gag Rule goes into effect, which tries to limit the number of antislavery petitions that reach Congress.
- In May Angelina Grimké writes *An Appeal to the Christian Women of the South* to instruct fellow Southern women to read, pray, speak, and act against the institution of slavery. Angelina says she felt "as if [God] directed and helped me to write it."
- In August Sarah Grimké writes *An Epistle to the Clergy of the Southern States*, which, based on scripture, said women as well as men had the right to fight for abolition.
- In November Angelina and Sarah attend the abolitionist agents' convention in New York where they are taught how to organize petitions and are trained in public speaking. They also meet Theodore Weld, the "lion of the tribe of abolitionists."

1837

- Maria Weston Chapman's book *Right and Wrong in Boston*, which was extremely critical of New England clergy, is published. Her sister Anne refers to it as a "spicey affair."
- In May Child, Mott, the Grimkés, and the Douglasses attend the first Anti-Slavery Convention of American Women in May in New York City. Eighty-one delegates from twelve states attend. They establish a national antislavery

petition campaign. Grace Douglass, Angelina Grimké, and Lydia Maria Child draft the *Appeal to the Women of the Nominally Free States*.

- Sarah and Angelina Grimké begin a widely successful speaking tour throughout the Northeast, addressing almost ninety audiences, in sixty-seven towns, to more than 40,000 people.
- A Pastoral Letter from the General Association of Congressional Ministers of Massachusetts to the Churches under Their Care is issued in July, stating, among other things, that women have a proper sphere as accorded to them in the New Testament. This creates a firestorm of debate.
- Oberlin College begins to accept female students.
- In October Abolitionist Samuel J. May gets over his "Pauline prejudice" against female abolitionists when he hears Angelina Grimké speak.

1838

- Sarah Douglass asks PFASS to take financial control of her all-girls' school so that she is no longer financially dependent on her parents.
- In February Angelina is the first woman to address the Committee of the Massachusetts House of Representatives, where she presents antislavery petitions on behalf of 20,000 women.
- In May Angelina Grimké marries Theodore Weld on the eve of the second Anti-Slavery Convention of American Women in a ceremony attended by black and white guests.
- The second Anti-Slavery Convention of American Women is held in May at Pennsylvania Hall in Philadelphia. A mob burns the hall down after the women leave.
- The New England Convention is held and states that women have no place in antislavery activities. A split occurs

between the feminist and antifeminist abolition societies in Massachusetts.
- Black women in Philadelphia organize the Female Vigilant Committee to support the Underground Railroad.
- The Welds open the Belleville School in New Jersey; many of their students are the children of abolitionists.

1839
- The third Anti-Slavery Convention of American Women is held in Philadelphia.
- *The Liberty Bell*, the successful antislavery annual edited by Maria Weston Chapman, is published by the Boston Female Anti-Slavery Society.
- The Massachusetts Female Emancipation Society, consisting of antifeminist abolitionists, is founded.

1840
- Sarah Douglass asks PFASS to relinquish financial control of her school, making it autonomous.
- The refusal to accept antislavery petitions becomes a standing rule of Congress, though John Quincy Adams notes that there were still "a greater number of petitions than at any former session."
- Catharine Beecher comes out against antislavery petitioning, which catalyzes a letter debate between her and Angelina Grimké.
- Child, Mott, and Maria Weston Chapman are elected to the executive committee of the AAS, their gender causing an uproar.
- Mott and her husband James attend the World's Anti-Slavery Convention in London. Though Lucretia is a delegate, she is excluded from participating in the convention. Women are allowed only as onlookers in the gallery.

Lucretia and Elizabeth Cady Stanton vow to take action to improve the position of women.
- The Manhattan Abolition Society is established by black women in New York.

1841
- Child is appointed editor of the *National Anti-Slavery Standard*; her husband, David Lee Child, becomes associate editor.

1842
- Grace Douglass dies.
- The Western New York Anti-Slavery Society (WNYASS), a mixed-sex society, is founded. The WNYASS is active in the Underground Railroad; many of its members will attend the first women's rights convention in Seneca Falls.

1848
- Mott visits the Seneca. From there, she goes to Seneca Falls, where she plans, with others, the first women's rights convention.

1849
- Sarah helps to organize the all-black Women's Association of 1849, whose goal was to support Frederick Douglass's cry for black nationalism.

1850
- Mott publishes *Discourse on Women*.

1853
- Sarah Douglass merges her girls' school with the Institute for Colored Youth. She will teach there for the next twenty years.

1861
- The Civil War erupts.
- Child works with Harriet Jacobs to publish *Incidents in the Life of a Slave Girl.*

1863
- The Emancipation Proclamation is promulgated.
- The Welds move to the Boston area to teach in a private school. They will live out their retirements in Massachusetts.

1864
- Mott helps to found Swarthmore College.

1865
- The Civil War ends.

1868
- Angelina Grimké Weld realizes that she and Sarah have three nephews from their brother's liaison with a slave. They assist two of the nephews, Archibald Henry and Francis James Grimké, who will do much for the civil rights movement, in obtaining an education.
- A group of one hundred and seventy-two women, including four black women, go to the town hall in Vineland, New Jersey, and "vote" ceremoniously.

1880
- In July Lydia Maria Child dies in Wayland, Massachusetts.
- In November Lucretia Mott dies and is acknowledged for her years of activism.

IMAGE PERMISSIONS

1. Fell, Margaret (1614-1702). *[Touch-stone. Part 2] Womens Speaking Justified . . .* (London, 1666), title page. Folger Shakespeare Library Shelfmark: F642 copy 1. Used by permission of the Folger Shakespeare Library under a Creative Commons Attribution-ShareAlike 4.0 International License.

2. Courtesy of the Library of Congress, LC-USZ61-1609 and LC-USZ61-1608.

3. Courtesy of the Library of Congress, LC-USZ62-42559.

4. Image credit: Quaker & Special Collections, Haverford College, Haverford, Pennsylvania.

5. Courtesy of the African American Registry.

6. Courtesy of the Boston Public Library.

7. "Collection of the Massachusetts Historical Society" Mary Grew, photograph by unidentified photographer, no date, Portraits of American Abolitionists, Massachusetts Historical Society.

8. "Collection of the Massachusetts Historical Society" Abby Kelley Foster, (1810–1887), photo. 81.248, photograph by unidentified photographer, no date, Portraits of American Abolitionists, Massachusetts Historical Society.

9. Image in the public domain.

10. Image in the public domain.

11. Image in the public domain.

12. Image in the public domain.

13. Courtesy of the Library of the Religious Society of Friends.

14. Courtesy of the Library of Congress, LC-USZ62-76081.

15. Image in the public domain.

16. Courtesy of the Library of Congress, LC-USZ62-1951.

17. Image credit: Sophia Smith Collection, Smith College.

HELEN LaKELLY HUNT, PhD, is a feminist donor activist. She cofounded several women's funds, including Women Moving Millions, and helped to spark the global women's philanthropy movement. She is the author of *Faith and Feminism* and coauthor of several best-selling books with her husband Harville Hendrix, with whom she developed Imago Relationship Therapy.

CORNEL WEST, PhD, is a prominent leftist American activist, social critic, and public intellectual. West is professor of philosophy and Christian practice at Union Theological Seminary, Professor Emeritus at Princeton University, and the author of more than twenty books.

The Feminist Press is a nonprofit educational organization founded to amplify feminist voices. FP publishes classic and new writing from around the world, creates cutting-edge programs, and elevates silenced and marginalized voices in order to support personal transformation and social justice for all people.

See our complete list of books at
feministpress.org